The Promise of
Paradox

OTHER BOOKS BY PARKER J. PALMER

The Promise of
Paradox

A Celebration of Contradictions
in the Christian Life

Parker J. Palmer

JOSSEY-BASS
A Wiley Imprint
www.josseybass.com

Published by Jossey-Bass
A Wiley Imprint
989 Market Street, San Francisco, CA 94103-1741—www.josseybass.com

Readers should be aware that Internet Web sites offered as citations and/or sources for further information may have changed or disappeared between the time this was written and when it is read.

Limit of Liability/Disclaimer of Warranty: While the publisher and author have used their best efforts in preparing this book, they make no representations or warranties with respect to the accuracy or completeness of the contents of this book and specifically disclaim any implied warranties of merchantability or fitness for a particular purpose. No warranty may be created or extended by sales representatives or written sales materials. The advice and strategies contained herein may not be suitable for your situation. You should consult with a professional where appropriate. Neither the publisher nor author shall be liable for any loss of profit or any other commercial damages, including but not limited to special, incidental, consequential, or other damages.

Jossey-Bass books and products are available through most bookstores. To contact Jossey-Bass directly call our Customer Care Department within the United States at (800) 956-7739, outside the United States at (317) 572-3986, or via fax at (317) 572-4002.

Jossey-Bass also publishes its books in a variety of electronic formats. Some content that appears in print may not be available in electronic books.

All biblical quotations are from the Revised Standard Version of the Bible, copyright © 1952, 1971, by the Division of Christian Education of the National Council of the Churches of Christ in the United States of America. Used by permission. All rights reserved.

"Man Is Born Tao," "The Empty Boat," "The Need to Win," and "The Woodcarver" by Thomas Merton, from THE WAY OF CHUANG TZU, copyright © 1965 by The Abbey of Gethsemani. Reproduced on behalf of the estate of Thomas Merton by kind permission of New Directions Publishing Corp. and Pollinger Limited.

Library of Congress Cataloging-in-Publication Data

Palmer, Parker J.
  The promise of paradox: a celebration of contradictions in Christian life / Parker Palmer – 3rd ed. ; foreword by Henri Nouwen – 3rd ed.
    p. cm.
  Includes bibliographical references.
  ISBN 9780787996963 (cloth)
    1. Spiritual life—Christianity.   2. Christian Communities I. Title.
BV4501.2 .P314 2008
248.4—dc19

Printed in the United States of America
FIRST EDITION
HB Printing 10 9 8 7 6 5 4 3 2 1

CONTENTS

GRATITUDES

My heartfelt thanks go to several people who helped bring this thirty-year-old book back to life. First and foremost, to Sheryl Fullerton, my editor at Jossey-Bass, who always sees more in my writing than I do and who surprised me one day by proposing this project. I'm ever grateful for her confidence, imagination, skill, and sense of humor.

Thanks, too, to Marcy Jackson, who read and commented astutely on the 2008 Introduction, and Sharon Palmer, who cast a keen editorial eye on the entire manuscript with her usual insight, care, and skill. Both of them helped me say what I wanted to say in the best way I know how.

Special thanks to my friends at the Servant Leadership School in Washington, D.C. The school was started in 1986 in the Adams Morgan neighborhood as an expression of the Church of the Saviour. The church, founded in 1947, was guided for decades by some of my heroes in the faith— Gordon Cosby, Mary Cosby, and Elizabeth O'Connor.

Shortly after Ave Maria Press let *The Promise of Paradox* go out of print, the Servant Leadership School offered to republish it. In gratitude and with deep respect for its work,

I assigned the copyright and all royalties from the book to the school. When Jossey-Bass suggested yet another republication, the folks at the school graciously returned the copyright to me.

If you want to know what kind of church the Church of the Saviour is or what kind of ministry the Servant Leadership School has, imagine Christianity at its very best, serving the least among us with profound humility and effectiveness, deeply rooted in its own faith tradition but radically open to the truth that is in others.

I am pleased that all royalties from this third incarnation of *The Promise of Paradox* will go to support the good work of the Servant Leadership School in the spirit of the Church of the Saviour. For more information or to make a gift to this important ministry, you may go to www.slschool.org, send e-mail to school@slschool.org, or call (202) 328-7312.

P.J.P.

INTRODUCTION
TO THE 1980 EDITION

Henri J. M. Nouwen

It is a real joy for me to introduce this first book by Parker Palmer. It is the joy that grows from friendship. I met Parker for the first time only five years ago and today I can hardly think of my life and work apart from the crucial role that Parker has played in them. The many hours we have spent eating together, playing together, dreaming together, talking together, studying together, reading together, writing together, and most of all praying together, have laid the basis for a supportive, nurturing and creative friendship.

This friendship has allowed me to see the pages of this book being born from Parker's own direct struggles with life and its many options and possibilities. Parker has shown me how true it is that you don't think your way into a new kind of living but live your way into a new kind of thinking. Every part of this book is a reflection of a new kind of living in which Parker and his family have engaged.

Parker's life story contains all the elements which contribute to making a well-known scholar: he studied theology, received a Ph.D. in sociology, taught at universities, did successful work as a community organizer, and wrote many remarkable articles. But this book is not the direct fruit of all of these accomplishments. On the contrary, it is the fruit of the many questions with which Parker bracketed these accomplishments. It is born out of the courageous and often agonizing critique of his own social, educational, and religious development.

This book is indeed the beautiful fruit of contradictions which became paradoxes: the contradiction between an educational success story and the growing need for simple community life; the contradiction between acceptance in respectable circles and the feeling of alienation and separation; the contradiction between speaking and lecturing about community and the loneliness of a highly individualized suburban existence; the contradiction between speaking more and more about religion and knowing God less and less. Parker lived these contradictions and tested them with his wife and children in spite of the cautionary voices surrounding him. Living these contradictions brought him to insights, ideas, and perspectives which could have been found in no other way.

This book is important not because it is written by a good scholar, but because it is written by a scholar who dared to wonder if his scholarship really led him to the truth. It is important not because it is written by a man who knows more than most people about the dynamics of community life, but because it is written by a man who gave up a large salary and moved away from a successful career to find community. It is important not because it is written by a man who has been a consultant to many on educational matters, but because it is written by a man who kept wondering if his own education didn't do him more harm than good and who gave much of his energy to a form of education not dominated by grades and degrees. It is important not because it is written by a man who knows the Bible well, but because it is written by a man who dared to let the Bible make radical claims on his own life and the lives of those he loves.

The way this book came about is the best testimony to its value. It came out of living the contradictions even when it was hard and painful to do so. This explains why the book does not offer one sustained argument; it contains six experiments in thinking which are all very radical in intent. I cannot read these pieces without wondering about my own life and without having to deal with my desire as well as resistance to move in the direction Parker points out.

The issues that Parker discusses are basic: solitude, community, social action, political responsibility, prayer, and contemplation. They are raised in the context of the words of William Johnston: "Faith is the breakthrough into that deep realm of the soul which accepts paradox . . . with humility." Accepting paradox with humility is the spirit that binds the quite diverse pieces of this book together. And it is the spirit that makes this book worth reading.

Parker Palmer has taught me much over the years. He has given me some very helpful concepts to work with; he has shown me how to think clearly and concisely; he has introduced me to many inspiring people and books. But most of all, he has challenged me by his own decisions to keep moving to unknown fields without apprehension or fear. He has taught me to live boldly and freely. That our many hours together can now be shared with others through this book is a source of great joy to me.

I hope and pray that those who read these essays will sense the spirit in which they were written and thus be challenged as I have been to break out of illusions and compulsions and seek a new freedom.

INTRODUCTION
TO THE 2008 EDITION

Parker J. Palmer

When my friends at Jossey-Bass said they wanted to reissue *The Promise of Paradox: A Celebration of Contradictions in the Christian Life*, I was delighted. Few things could make a writer happier than knowing that his first book, a book with real age on it, still has legs. At the same time, I knew that revisiting *Promise* thirty years after publishing it would be both a blessing and a curse.

The curse seemed clear to me. Preparing this new edition would require me to compare what I believed at age forty to what I believe today. And that, I thought, might be awkward. The first edition of *Promise* has an author photo of such studied intensity that it embarrasses me, though I do admire—OK, envy—that young man's big hair. What if some of my 1980 convictions proved as embarrassing as that photo? What if I felt unable to explain them to myself, let alone to my readers? In particular, how would I deal with the way my relationship to Christianity has changed from my first book to my most recent?

The Promise of Paradox has a lot of Christian language in it, from its subtitle to chapters on the way of the cross and the politically incorrect apostle Paul. But the books I've written in the last decade or so—*A Hidden Wholeness*, *Let Your Life Speak*, and *The Courage to Teach*—rarely use the word God and never speak of Jesus, and not by accident.

I've worked hard for a long time to find a language about the inner life that builds bridges, not walls, and today I am grateful to have both Christian and non-Christian readers. I am especially grateful for readers like Richard Hughes who bridge that gap with open-mindedness and insight. Hughes, a longtime professor of history at Pepperdine University, now at Messiah College, wrote about my book, *The Courage to Teach*:

> Parker Palmer has written a book that appears to be—and, in fact, in many ways is—a secular text for a secular audience on a secular topic: the improvement of classroom teaching. At the same time, this text draws so profoundly on the riches of the Quaker tradition that I am forced to regard it as one of the finest examples of Christian scholarship that I have encountered. I regard the book in this way not because it promotes itself as a Christian text, since most certainly it does not, but rather because its secular content draws strength and power from a Christian vision of reality.[1]

Richard Hughes understands my method and my madness. But as I contemplated reissuing *Promise*, it seemed unlikely to me that I would fare so well with all of my readers as I traced my changed relationship to Christianity over the past thirty years. My non-Christian readers might not like where I came from, my Christian readers might not like where I've been going, and this could create what is known in the book biz as a "marketing problem."

I'll return to that little problem later, after I explore some of the blessings this project has brought me. I've learned that I deal better with curses when I remind myself that blessings abound, just as I deal better with my shadows when I remember that forgiveness is real.

Working on these pages has given me a chance to reconnect in memory and meaning with people, places, and events that were formative in my life. It has allowed me to give thanks once again for those miraculously graced friendships and experiences without which my life would have been unspeakably poorer. And as often happens when I am willing to take the risk, I have found blessing laced through what I anticipated might be pure curse.

Revisiting what I believed as a forty-year-old—and retracing the spiritual journey that took me from then to now—has helped me, as I approach age seventy, to get ready to take next steps. Check with me thirty years from now, and I'll let you know what those next steps turned out to be.

Blessings Abound

Whatever its flaws in substance and style—and I found a few!—*The Promise of Paradox* will always be dear to me, in the way I hold dear all the generous people who opened doors for me along the way. It's not that *Promise* launched me as a writer. By age forty, I had been writing short pieces for nearly twenty years and had even published a few. But *Promise* proved that I could write a book despite my conviction that I could not—and did so even as I clung to that belief. And therein lies a tale.

In the spring of 1978, I was dean of studies at Pendle Hill, the Quaker adult study center near Philadelphia.[2] I was teaching a course on Thomas Merton and had rented a film of Merton's last talk for our final session. A week before the end of term, I called the Abbey of Gethsemane to ask when the film would arrive, only to learn that the movie monk had double-booked it and sent it to the other place. (That's when I realized that Merton was not blowing smoke when he complained that even monasteries have bureaucratic screw-ups!)

Wanting to bring the class to a fitting conclusion, I spent the next few days writing a lecture on Merton's spirituality of paradox, a theme that runs through his work. I hardly ever write out lectures word for word, preferring the freedom of speaking from an outline, but this time I broke my own rule. One of my students asked for a copy of the talk, saying that her uncle, a Catholic priest, had a great interest in Merton. A month or so later, an editor at Ave Maria Press, a small Catholic publishing house in Notre Dame, Indiana, called. My student's uncle had sent him my talk, and he wondered if I'd let Ave Maria publish it in its monthly newsletter. Of course, I gladly said yes.

After a few months, the editor called again to say that reader response to my piece had been enthusiastic. "Do you have any more essays lying around, especially related to paradox?" When I told him that I had been filling file drawers with essays for years, he asked me to send him a dozen or so. A month later, he called a third time to say that he thought six of my pieces could be arranged in a book. Would I be willing to sign a contract?

In a moment of satori worthy of a Zen wannabe, I realized that not only could I write a book, I already had! It was a great reminder of the first lesson in Spirituality 101: *Pay attention!* You may discover that what you wanted is right in front of you, a secret hidden in plain sight.

The Promise of Paradox was an accidental book. But once I held a copy in my hands, I knew I could write more books if I wanted to. Apparently I did. *The Company of Strangers* came out in 1981 and *To Know as We Are Known* in 1983. After that breathless sprint, I began to write at a more sustainable pace, with four more books over the next twenty-five years.

Closely tied in memory to the launch of my book-writing career is my friendship with Henri Nouwen, who wrote the

Introduction to *Promise*. I met Henri in the mid-seventies, a couple of years before the book was published. We were among a small group of people called together by the Lilly Endowment for a consultation on spirituality, a notion that was just beginning to attract mainstream attention. We spent three days in New York's Algonquin Hotel evaluating dozens of grant proposals. All of the judges emerged with generous stipends for their time, and some of the applicants emerged with handsome grants. But I emerged with something far more precious: a friendship with Henri that animated a decade of shared work.

When I met Henri, he was already a well-known and much-loved writer. His classic *Reaching Out: The Three Movements of the Spiritual Life* (1975) had touched me and many other readers.[3] Henri was only seven years older than I, but to me, he seemed like a wise older brother, a virtuoso of the spiritual life with a genius for writing and teaching. He was also very funny, a requisite quality for any guru who hopes to win my trust.

Given my high regard for Henri and my insecurity as a writer, it was with fear and trembling that I asked if he would help put my accidental book on the map by writing an introduction. Henri immediately said, "Yes, of course," an answer he gave many people on many occasions. A month later, he sent me several pages that I read over and over again, hardly able to believe that those words of affirmation were about me.

Today I understand that those words are only partly about me. They are also about Henri Nouwen's open and generous heart. His death in 1996 at the far-too-young age of sixty-five means that a lot of us need to step up to replace the generosity lost to the universe when that heart stopped beating.

To round out this recounting of blessings, the reissuing of *Promise* has helped me revisit one of the most transformative periods of my life, my eleven-year sojourn at Pendle Hill. Founded in 1930, this Quaker adult study center is organized as a residential community where some seventy people share a daily round of worship, study, physical work, and shared decision making—a place that has elements of a kibbutz, an ashram, a monastery, a zendo, and on occasion, a madhouse. It is also a place where I received powerful and lasting lessons about the inner journey, the kind of community that supports it, and the way such a journey rightly taken returns us to caring for the needs of the world.

In 1975, when I began working at Pendle Hill as dean of studies, my salary was $2,400 a year, the equivalent of about $10,000 in 2008. In addition, my family and I received free room and board, a very helpful supplement to the cash, but even so, not what a person with a Ph.D. from Berkeley would expect to be making then or now. Back in the day, everyone on staff at Pendle Hill received the same compensation package, including an eighteen-year-old with a high school diploma who worked in the garden, the shop, or the kitchen. It was communism Quaker-style, and to a white male who had grown up on Chicago's affluent North Shore, it was a challenge.

Every member of the Pendle Hill staff had a daily job related to one of the meals, either preparing it or cleaning up afterward. My qualifications for dishwashing were weak but much stronger than my gifts for food preparation. So for eleven years, luncheon cleanup was my afternoon delight. As dean, I had to be on the road from time to time, raising money or giving a talk. But like everyone else at Pendle Hill, I had to line up a sub whenever I missed a meal job and then repay that person by doing his or her job as well as my own for as many days as I had been gone. If you can name a dean of anything who currently lives under such a stricture, I will gladly volunteer to do his or her dishes for a day!

And what did Pendle Hill's salary scale and work program have to do with those powerful and lasting spiritual lessons I mentioned? Well, it's all right there: a setup that slammed me into my narcissistic feelings of entitlement, step one on the inner journey for a lot of folks like me; a form of community that not only forced such issues on me but offered disciplines (like shared silence and gentle truth-telling) for dealing with them; and a way of life that deepened my solidarity with people who live with little not by choice but because of economic injustice. These, I daresay, are different from the spiritual challenges that I would have faced had I taken a job at some university.

Remembering all of that is, for me, much more than a trip down memory lane. It is a true blessing, an opportunity as I near age seventy to reclaim and recommit to what I know to be true about myself and my world.

Curses!

As I reread this book, two things jumped out at me. First, there are many pages where I would not change a word were I to write about the same topic today, in part because I still believe what those words say and in part because I don't know how to say it any better. Second, there are pages in this book that I would not write today, and I feel a bit squeamish about allowing them to be republished. I am doing so largely because I believe that my forty-year-old self has as much right to freedom of speech as the sixty-nine-year-old version![4]

My squeamishness has little to do with any fundamental change in my beliefs. I still understand myself as a Christian, and many traditional Christian understandings still shape my life. But in 2008, I find it hard to name my beliefs using traditional Christian language because that vocabulary has been taken hostage by theological terrorists and tortured beyond recognition. Of course, this is not the first time Christian rhetoric has been violated in public places. But the violence I'm talking about is happening right here and right now, and the wounds—my wounds—are very raw.

I would be lost in the dark without the light Christianity sheds on my life, the light I find in truths like incarnation, grace, sacrament, forgiveness, blessing, and the paradoxical dance of death and resurrection. But when Christians claim that their light is the only light and that anyone who does not share their understanding of it is doomed to eternal damnation, things get very dark for me. I want to run screaming out into the so-called secular world—which is, I believe, better-named the wide, wild world of God—where I can recover my God-given mind.

Out there, I catch sight once again of the truth, goodness, and beauty that disappear when pious Christians slam the door on their musty, windowless, lifeless room. Next to a Christian eclipsed by theological arrogance, an honest atheist shines like the sun. Next to a church profaned by its exclusion of "otherness," a city of true diversity is a cathedral.

How can it be that Christianity—named after one who proclaimed that "the meek shall inherit the earth"—can give rise to so much arrogance? Here, for example, is a scenario that gets played out a lot these days. A man born into wealth and power spends the first twenty years of his adult life as a wastrel and a rake, kept afloat by privilege rather than his own work and wit. Then he encounters Christ, stops drinking, and starts getting serious about *something*—maybe politics, for example.

I am happy for him. Happy until it becomes clear that this man has emerged from his encounter believing that God speaks clearly and directly to him about all things; that whatever conclusions he comes to "in prayer" are divinely inspired and binding on others; and that the outcomes of his God-inspired decisions are always right, even in the face of overwhelming evidence to the contrary.

Let us suppose that this man's newfound seriousness, fueled by his family's connections and wealth, leads to political success, and he suddenly has access to real power. Given what he believes about his own corner on truth, I would sooner see him start drinking again. As moral problems go, one person's alcoholism is not nearly as serious as the social, economic, and political damage such a delusional leader can do, all in the name of God. If he stays in office long enough, part of that damage is called "creeping totalitarianism."

If I had been on a journey like this man's—and I have, of course; who hasn't had to be saved from oneself in one way or another?—my take-home lesson would be simple: "I'm capable of making really big mistakes, like being a callow and witless nincompoop for the first two decades of my adult life. Now that I've been given another chance, I must live with appropriate humility."

How does someone meet the grandeur and grace of God in Christ, get saved from his own smallness, and emerge from the experience cocky instead of humble? I can think of only two answers: either he did not meet the Real Deal but a cheap imitation thereof, or he met the Real Deal and blew a chance to be saved. Fortunately, that chance comes again and again, even to nincompoops like him. And me.

Yes, I believe in forgiveness, grace, salvation (which means becoming whole), and in the Word made flesh (which I believe everyone is). In fact, the major convictions of Christian faith are much more than "articles of belief" for me. They are lenses on life that have helped me make sense of myself, a person I find at least as baffling as the fellow I've just described.

Having gone over to the dark side three times with major clinical depression and lived to tell the tale, the cross, death-and-resurrection, and grace are familiar landmarks on the terrain called my life. For me, the Christian story is neither a fairy tale (as it is sometimes portrayed by disbelievers) nor an ought-ridden morality play (as it is sometimes portrayed by believers). It is simply an honest, terrifying, bracing, and ultimately reassuring way of telling it like it is.

I am not sure I could live without this powerful way of naming and negotiating reality as I know it. But I know for a certainty that I cannot live with the way some Christians and their churches deploy this power. How can a person believe in the grace of God and still believe that God's grace is available only to folks who sign up for a particular understanding of how God works in our lives—*their* particular understanding?

When Christians answer that question by saying, "God caused Jesus to die on the cross as atonement for the sins of humanity, so if you want salvation, you must believe in Jesus Christ," my question ratchets up. What kind of God is it who demands blood—the blood of *God's own son*—for atonement? I'm a father myself, and sure, in moments of hurt and rage, I've wanted to "kill" my kids a time or two. But always for *their* sins, not yours. I don't want a God to whom I can feel morally superior. And I don't want a theology that advocates blood sacrifice as a way of setting things right. There's way too much of that going around these days.

Jesus died on the cross because he got crosswise with the powers that be, a story that has been repeated time and again in human history. For me, his death is redemptive not because it fulfills the puppet master's plan or works some kind of cosmic sleight of hand but because it represents God's willingness to suffer with us in every moment of our lives, not least when we are willing to speak truth to power. That's the meaning of the word *compassion*—"suffering with"—a source of supreme comfort and a gift God gives us so we can pass it on to others. And thank God, Jesus is only one among many embodiments of that gift: the world has endless need for incarnations of compassion.

Think of the Buddhists in war-torn Vietnam or currently in exile from Tibet, bearing the suffering that comes from being victims of violence but committed to a nonviolent campaign for justice and peace that extends compassion to their enemies. Looked at through Christian lenses, they are "Christ-like." But they have every right to look back at this "Christian nation"—remembering how our warplanes napalmed Vietnamese children or watching as we turn a blind eye toward Tibet—and ask themselves, "Is this *really* what Jesus would do?"

When I was growing up in the church, I was grabbed by a biblical quote that I internalized as follows (a composite from several translations, as it turns out, but a reasonably accurate rendering): "We have this treasure in earthen vessels to show that the transcendent power belongs to God and not to us" (2 Corinthians 4:7). That line explains two things: why I find theological arrogance profoundly unchristian and why I still have some hope in the Christian community's capacity to correct itself.

These earthen vessels—the containers that hold and convey the mysteries of faith—include every word in our scriptures and theologies, every doctrine in our creeds, every structure that holds up the institutional church. The pope, the doctrine of atonement, the word *God* itself—all of them are clay pots, prone to crack and leak, crumble and break. And that's a good thing because it reminds us we are embedded in a truth so vast that our mental constructs can never comprehend it; because it cultivates the humility required to look at that mystery through other people's eyes, giving us a chance to learn more about it; because it keeps us from becoming theological fascists.

At least, that's the theory. In practice, it's a very small step from cracked pots to crackpots. Too many Christians believe that their thoughts about God and God's thoughts are the same thing. Anne Lamott has a good response for such folks when they insist that her brand of Christianity is a one-way ticket to hell. She thanks them for sharing and then says, "You know the difference between you and God? God *never* thinks He's you."[5]

As far as I can tell, a person who believes that he or she speaks God's truth in pure, unadulterated form—or believes that some other mortal being speaks that way (e.g., one of the folks whose words ended up in the Bible)—is an idolater, a person who worships false gods, the false gods of human formulation. I want to say to them, "Neither your concept of God nor mine is the same as God. It says so in the Bible, and it's just plain common sense. So we should learn to talk to each other in hopes of understanding God—maybe even each other—a little more deeply."

If I am wrong about this, I hope someone will prove me wrong before it is too late. Until then, I will continue to have a love-hate relationship with any church that spawns and feeds idolaters who compound their sin by condemning to hell anyone who sees things differently. I don't believe that these idolaters are headed for an eternity of torment, and I certainly don't wish that for them. They are making things hellish right now, and what I wish is that they would get a life.

What's Promising About Paradox?

When Thomas Merton was novice master at the Abbey of Gethsemane, his sessions were often taped. He started off one class by speaking these words to the earnest and pious would-be monks who'd been placed in his care: "Men, before you can have a spiritual life, you've got to have a life!"

I treasure that line because it sheds the light of humor on one of the big problems of both religion and spirituality: the assumption that the spiritual life is a life set apart from "secular" life—which is to say, from the life one is living.

My guess is that Merton's comment created a two-wave response in some of his listeners: "Wow, he's right, I need to get a life! No, wait a minute, I've already got one—but it's that god-awful mess I tried to leave behind when I came to the monastery!"

Merton's point, of course, is that we will find our spiritual lives in that mess itself, in its earthy realities, unpredictable challenges, surprising resources, creative dynamics. I think he would approve of the proposal that we add a new prayer to the well-known short list of "Thanks!" and "Help!" The new one is equally simple: "Bless this mess!"

If we stand in the middle of the mess assuming that the spiritual life will be orderly and pristine, linear and logical, without complexity or contradiction, we will pray not for a blessing but for an extreme makeover. Of course, the ultimate extreme makeover is an embalmed and well-accessorized corpse, which is what we become in life when we try to defy the wideness and wildness of God.

I believe God wants us to be good, but above all God wants us to be alive: life, after all, is God's original gift to us. To try to put that gift back in the box so it can be retied and shelved is to stick your finger in the eye of the giver. And when Christians use their conception of "goodness" to diminish or destroy other people's lives, either figuratively or literally—as when they declare homosexuals unholy or use God to justify warfare against innocent civilians—they stick fingers in both of God's eyes.

I don't deny the importance of moral order, an order that can only be created by dialogue, not dictation. (Dictating morality is a sin against our God-given freedom, and you can't get moral order out of an immoral process.) But if disorder is not as important as order, how are we to understand what drives personal and social creativity and evolution? As I said to a friend recently, "Why do people think getting 'centered' is such a great thing? I find myself most drawn to 'eccentric' or off-center people because they are interesting and flat-out fun!"

The promise of paradox is the promise that apparent opposites—like order and disorder—can cohere in our lives, the promise that if we replace either-or with both-and, our lives will become larger and more filled with light. It is a promise at the heart of every wisdom tradition I know, not least the Christian faith. How else can I make sense of the statement "If you seek your life, you will lose it, but if you lose your life, you will find it"? Or "The first shall be last and the last shall be first"? Or the affirmation that Jesus Christ was fully human and fully divine? Or the notion that we know there is a God but we cannot claim to know the God that is?

The dictionary defines a paradox as "a statement that seems self-contradictory or absurd but in reality expresses a possible truth." Neils Bohr, the Nobel Prize–winning physicist, says essentially the same thing with the most lucid words I've read on the subject: "The opposite of a correct statement is a false statement. But the opposite of a profound truth may be another profound truth."[6]

It is important to note that little phrase "may be." Not all apparent contradictions are paradoxes in disguise, so discernment is required. The Orwellian slogan "War Is Peace" does not qualify, no matter how many presidents say otherwise. But the fact that we are made for solitude *and* for community is a true paradox, one that we fail to embrace at our peril.

The capacity to embrace true paradoxes is more than an intellectual skill for holding complex thoughts. It is a life skill for holding complex experiences. Take, for example, our encounter with "the other," with the person who sees a different reality from ours because he or she stands in a different place. To some extent, the other contradicts not only our thoughts but also our lives, and that can be threatening. If we lack the capacity to allow this contradiction to segue into a paradox—a both-and that has the potential to open our minds and hearts to something new—we will most likely fall back on our hard-wired "fight or flight" response. But if we understand the promise of paradox, our encounters with "the other" have the potential to make our world larger, more generous, more hopeful.

Or take the experience I call "standing in the tragic gap." From international relations to what goes on in the workplace to raising a teenager, we find ourselves living between reality and possibility, between what is and what could and should be. But if we are willing actively to "hang in there" with a country, a colleague, or a child—holding the unresolved tension between reality and possibility and inviting something new into being—we have a chance to participate in the evolution of a better reality.

Standing in the gap is challenging, but the alternatives are irresponsible. One is to fall out on the side of too much reality and into corrosive cynicism. The other is to fall out on the side of too much possibility and into irrelevant idealism. Both take us out of the action. But if we are willing to stand between the poles, refusing to fall out, we have a chance to play a life-giving role in the development of a child, a workplace, or a world that needs to grow into "the better angels of its nature."

If we are to stand in the gap, we need to know the promise of paradox—and know it in a way that goes deeper than intellect, a way suggested by one of the most famous lines of biblical poetry: "The Word became flesh and dwelt among us, full of grace and truth" (John 1:14). I believe that those words, written to describe Jesus, name what all are called to do: wrap our whole selves around the truth given to us and live it out in our embodied lives.

For many years, I've asked a simple question about any idea that seems life-giving to me: "How can we put wheels on that idea?" It's an inelegant rendition of "the Word become flesh," but it works for me. And in the thirty years since this book was published, I've had some experience at putting wheels on the idea of paradox, taking myself and others into a lived experience of holding tension in ways that open our hearts and minds to something new and unexpected.

To take one example, people can experience the promise of paradox—or not—in the way churches and other communities make collective decisions. When we make decisions by majority rule, we deprive people of the chance to learn how to hold tension creatively. Under these ground rules, we are encouraged to "resolve" the tension between opposing views by taking a vote and getting it over with (although in practice, the lingering resentment of the losing side can undermine forward movement for a long time thereafter).

But when we make decisions by consensus—when we cannot proceed until everyone is willing to do so—people must learn to listen to those they disagree with in a new way. Now the question is not "How can I win the vote by persuading enough people that you are wrong?" but "How might I learn from your truth in a way that enlarges my understanding and express my truth in a way that expands yours?"

Under the ground rules of consensus, we are encouraged to hold the tension of apparently contradictory viewpoints—and we often find ourselves happily surprised at the new and larger truth that emerges as a result. That is the promise of paradox.

A Concluding Postscript

As I reread *The Promise of Paradox*, I was startled to discover how many of the questions I am working on today are the same ones I was working on thirty years ago. Paradox itself pops up in every book I've written, and there it is again in an essay I've been sketching out while writing this Introduction.

I can think of several explanations for this fact. One: I'm a fundamentally boring person who is stuck in a rut. Two: I am one of those writers who have only one book in them, a book they rewrite many times. Three: we are born with a core of personal identity that persists to the day we die, so our fundamental questions remain unchanged. I'm going to go with the third explanation because it is the most dignified.

For years, I've wanted a bumper sticker that says "Born Baffled!" I've come to believe that the willingness to be baffled and stay baffled is part of my identity and one of my birthright gifts. I mean "gift" seriously: bafflement has energized my life, including my work as a writer. Writers are sometimes regarded as experts on the subjects they write about. But I've never written on a topic that I've mastered or figured out. Once I arrive at what some might call expertise, I get bored, and writing is hard enough without working on something I find boring. I write about things that baffle me even after I've written about them, which is to say that I write about things whose mystery seems bottomless to me.

Early on, my bafflement was focused on the world and how it does or does not work. Then it came to rest on other people: Why are they the way they are? Finally, I realized that the root of all bafflement is about oneself and that unless I was willing to become more transparent to myself, other people and the world would remain opaque.

So at bottom, my longtime fascination with paradox is rooted in my longtime bafflement about myself. As I wrote thirty years ago on the first page of *Promise:*

> Contradiction, paradox, the tension of opposites: these have always been at the heart of my experience, and I think I am not alone. I am tugged one way and then the other. My beliefs and my actions often seem at odds. My strengths are sometimes canceled by my weaknesses. My self, and the world around me, seem more a study in dissonance than a harmony of the integrated whole.

I've made some progress toward personal integration over the past thirty years, helped along by the concept of paradox. But there is still much truth about me in that paragraph, and there always will be—at least, as long as I am fully engaged with life. Which is why I continue to find solace in Thomas Merton's words: "Like Jonas himself I find myself traveling toward my destiny in the belly of a paradox."

Jonas, or Jonah, is the fellow who was famously swallowed by a whale, lived to tell the tale, and for his troubles got written up in the Bible. He was trying to escape God's calling when the crew of his getaway ship tossed him overboard in the whale's neighborhood. But instead of snacking, the whale swallowed Jonah whole and took him to Nineveh, the very place to which God had called Jonah in the first place. The moral of the story is yet another paradox: running away from a true calling may be the surest way to run toward it, even though you may arrive soaked and smelly.

The perils of such a flight, of course, are very real. For years I've had an original woodcut by Fritz Eichenberg in my office. Eighteen inches high and nearly twelve inches wide, it tells the Jonah story in a sequence of images running from the top to the bottom of the piece. The depiction is dark and tumultuous, full of leviathans, roiled seas, and high drama, and at the bottom, it shows Jonah safe ashore. For me, this woodcut is an image of what it's been like from time to time to navigate the ocean of life, struggling with my callings as both a public and a private person, resisting and yielding, drowning and surfacing, but somehow being led.

In the middle of the woodcut, left of center, is an all-seeing eye full of light that pierces the darkness. It is surely the eye of God, an eye that has always been on Jonah—an eye that will, as they say, "see him through." There's a nice double meaning to those words: God sees through Jonah, through his illusions and delusions, and God will stay with Jonah to and through the end.

Of course, none of this seems plausible when you are in midflight, being tossed overboard, or swallowed up into the dark belly of the beast. But when you arrive at that distant shore and have a chance to catch your breath, spiff up, and look around, it begins to become clear that something has been leading you all along.

Looking at Eichenberg's woodcut, it seems clear that it would make no sense artistically to portray this light-filled eye in the middle of a scene where, say, a couple of well-cushioned gents enjoying a well-heeled retirement are strolling down the fairway toward the nineteenth hole. The image works only because of the challenging backdrop against which it is set, only because it completes the paradox of darkness and light, blindness and sight. I hate to reduce the promise of paradox to a line from a 1950s pop song, but it's just plain true that "you can't have one without the other."

It's not so much that "you can have it all" as that you must embrace it all, if you want life in the round. Margaret Fuller, the nineteenth-century New England transcendentalist, reputedly said, "I accept the universe!" To which the essayist Thomas Carlyle is said to have responded, "Gad! she'd better!"[7]

That's a great quip, but Fuller really did have a choice. Instead of accepting, she could have rejected the complexity and contradictions of life, trying—as many people and belief systems, secular as well as religious, do—to reduce it to a few variables to create the illusion that things are simple and we are in charge.

But that kind of thinking leads us to a world of grief. Witness, even as I write, American involvement in Iraq. Here is grief multiplied by a million, and the math that kicked it off was premised in the American assumption that the complexities of that region could be simplified by our military might, never mind Vietnam or all the other wars we have failed to win since 1945. If we had been able to hold the paradoxical complexity of the fact that the human heart sometimes yearns both for the sweet air of freedom *and* for the order, however oppressive, that a dictatorship brings, we might have been less cocksure about our mission and more constructive in response to our national dilemma and Iraqi realities.

When you are traveling toward your destiny in the belly of a paradox, as we all are, there are no certainties. But the creative opportunities are boundless. Resist that fact, and life can get brutal. Embrace it, and life becomes one whale of a ride.

for Sally

The Promise of
Paradox

CHAPTER I

In the Belly of a Paradox

In 1953, in his twelfth year as a Trappist monk, Thomas Merton published a journal of his days called *The Sign of Jonas*. Fifteen years later, when I first read his preface, I knew I had been touched by a teacher and a friend:

> The sign Jesus promised to the generation that did not understand him was the "sign of Jonas the prophet"—that is, the sign of his own resurrection. The life of every . . . Christian is signed with the sign of Jonas because we all live by the power of Christ's resurrection. But I feel that my own life is especially sealed with this great sign . . . because like Jonas himself I find myself traveling toward my destiny in the belly of a paradox.[1]

Here is Merton's writing at its best, sturdy with religious conviction but laced with wit and fresh images of the religious life. That would have been enough for me, but I was drawn by substance as well as style, by the idea of life as a whale of a paradox.

Contradiction, paradox, the tension of opposites: these have always been at the heart of my experience, and I think I am not alone. I am tugged one way and then the other. My beliefs and my actions often seem at odds. My strengths are sometimes canceled by my weaknesses. My self, and the world around me, seem more a study in dissonance than a harmony of the integrated whole.

More than once have I despaired at the corrosive effect of these contradictions on my "spiritual life." I had thought that living spiritually required a resolution of all contraries and tensions before one could hope, as it were, to earn one's wings. But as I labored to remove the contradictions before presenting myself to God, my spiritual life became a continual preliminary attraction, never quite getting to the main event. I thought I was living in the spirit by railing against life's inconsistencies when in fact I was becoming more frustrated, more anxious, more withdrawn from those vital places in life where contradiction always lurks.

For me, there was light and liberation in Merton's image of life in the belly of a paradox. Perhaps one need not resolve life's contradictions single-handedly. Perhaps one could be swallowed up by paradox and still be delivered to the shores of one's destiny—even as was Jonah from the belly of the whale. Perhaps contradictions are not impediments to the spiritual life but an integral part of it. Through them we may learn that the power for life comes from God, not from us.

Thomas Merton was well qualified to teach us about contradiction and paradox. He was a monk vowed to solitude and silence who wrote more than sixty books and became an international figure in his own time. He withdrew from the pace and demands of worldly life to pray among Kentucky's wooded hills and yet saw prophetically into racism and militarism and became patron saint of social activists. A Roman Catholic whose early writings are sometimes too parochial for my taste, he became a universal religious figure, steeped in Taoism and Zen, hailed by some in the East as an incarnate Buddha.

In the midst of his contradictions, Merton found the grace of God, and that discovery is a gift to all of us whose lives are pulled between the poles. In the preface to a collection of his essays, Merton writes:

> I have had to accept the fact that my life is almost totally paradoxical. I have also had to learn gradually to get along without apologizing for the fact, even to myself. And perhaps this preface is an indication that I have not yet completely learned. No matter. It is in the paradox itself, the paradox which was and is still a source of insecurity, that I have come to find the greatest security. I have become convinced that the very contradictions in my life are in some ways signs of God's mercy to me; if only because someone so complicated and so prone to confusion and self-defeat could hardly survive for long without special mercy.[2]

In this essay, I want to explore and celebrate some contradictions in Merton's thought and see what he has to teach us about our own.

Contradiction, Paradox, and the Life of the Spirit

The contradictions of life are not accidental. Nor do they result from inept living. They are inherent in human nature and in the circumstances that surround our lives. We are, as the Psalmist says, "little less than God" but also "like the beasts that perish" (Psalms 8:5; 49:12). Our highest insights and aspirations fail because we are encumbered by flesh that is too weak—or too strong. When we rise to soar on wings of spirit, we discover weights of need and greed tied to our feet. The things we seek consciously and with effort tend to evade us, while our blessings come quietly and unbidden. When we achieve what we most want, our pleasure in it often fades.

These contradictions of private life are multiplied over and over when we enter the public world of work and politics. Here is a realm where values cancel each other out: how, for example, can we simultaneously have freedom and equality? Here, as a million factions compete for scarce resources, vision yields to compromise, which is the law of collective survival, or to the law of nature red in tooth and claw. Here is a self-negating world where our finest achievements may yield negative by-products: medical science lengthens human life only to increase starvation in some societies and draw out the agonies of aging in others.

Beyond the private and public worlds are contradictions we might call cosmic that implicate even God, the religious conundrums that have bedeviled men and women for millennia. If God is loving, all-knowing, and omnipotent, why is there evil in the universe? And why do the wicked sometimes flourish while the virtuous wither? At every level of our lives, we are stretched and torn between opposites that seem irreconcilable, discouraging, defeating.

Thomas Merton understood that the way we respond to contradiction is pivotal to our spiritual lives. The moments when we meet and reckon with contradiction are turning points where we either enter or evade the mystery of God. After all, this is the God who said, "I form light and create darkness, I make weal and create woe" (Isaiah 45:7). It is a statement that Christians seldom take seriously, preferring to blame the Devil for all the darkness and woe.

We embark on the spiritual journey in hopes of achieving wholeness, but long before we get there, the journey only sharpens and magnifies our sense of contradiction. The truth of the Spirit contradicts the lies we are living. The light of the Spirit contradicts our inner shadow-life. The unity of the Spirit contradicts our brokenness.

For some of us, the tension between Spirit and self is so great that we abandon the spiritual quest: we turn away from the source and walk in shadows because we do not want to see ourselves in an unbecoming light. Some of us resolve the tension by denying our own darkness and trying to walk where the lights are on all the time: we hold the dark world at bay and seek out situations that satisfy our need to stay "pure." In one way or another, we remove ourselves from the great dramas of life where God and world interact, where light and dark cohere, where contradiction abounds.

But there is a third way to respond, a way beyond choosing either this pole or that: let us call it "living the contradictions." Here we refuse to flee from tension but allow that tension to occupy the center of our lives. And why would we want to do that? Because by doing so, we may receive one of the great gifts of the spiritual life, *the transformation of contradiction into paradox*. The poles of either-or, the choices we thought we had to make, may become signs of a larger truth than we had even dreamed—and in that truth, our lives may become larger than we ever imagined possible.

A contradiction, says the *Oxford English Dictionary*, is a statement containing elements logically at variance with one another. A paradox is a statement that seems self-contradictory but on investigation may prove to be essentially true. The insights of many wisdom traditions would be judged contra- dictions by the norms of conventional logic. But by spiritual norms, these insights contain paradoxical truth:

> He who finds his life will lose it, and he who loses his life for my sake will find it. (Matthew 10:34)

Before I grasped Zen, the mountains were nothing but mountains and the rivers nothing but rivers. When I got into Zen, the mountains were no longer mountains and the rivers no longer rivers. But when I understood Zen, the mountains were only mountains and the rivers only rivers. (Zen saying)[3]

Love is something if you give it away, you'll end up having more! (popular song)[4]

Spiritual truth often seems self-contradictory when judged by conventional logic. Where logic wants to separate and divide, the seeker looks for what Merton called life's "hidden wholeness," the underlying unity of all things. Logic assumes that whatever violates the rules of rationality cannot possibly be true. Spirituality assumes that the deeper our questions go, the less useful those rules become. The spiritual life—whose territory is the nonrational, not the irrational—proceeds with a trembling confidence that God's truth is too large for the simplicity of either-or. It can be apprehended only by the complexity of both-and.

But before I move on, a word or two of warning. By lifting up the promise of paradox, I do not intend to endorse the simpleminded view that all truth is relative, that there are no critical differences between true and false, right and wrong. That kind of silliness weakens the idea of paradox, whose promise comes partly from the fact that the world is full of very real opposites pulling vigorously against each other, opposites that can never be resolved into paradoxes. We appreciate paradox not by abandoning our critical faculties but by sharpening them.

I have heard the term *paradox* used as if it were an incantation that could magically remove life's tensions and relieve us of responsibility for them. I have heard people use the word to describe the gap between behavior and belief as if the word itself would excuse and even sanctify the contradiction, allowing us to forget about it. But that is what Bonhoeffer called "cheap grace," and nothing could be further from Merton's understanding or mine.

Our first need is not to release the tension but to *live the contradictions*, fully and painfully aware of the poles between which our lives are stretched. As we do so, we will be plunged into paradox, at whose heart we will find transcendence and new life. Our lives will be changed; our beliefs and our actions will become more responsive to God's spirit. But this will happen only as we become engulfed by contradictions that God alone can resolve. With Jonah, we will be delivered, but only if we allow ourselves to be swallowed into darkness.

Just as Thomas Merton helps us understand ourselves through contradiction and paradox, so those principles help us understand his thought. In hopes of achieving both goals, I want to look at Merton's treatment of three topics: Marxism, Taoism, and the way of the cross. Though these would seem to be contradictory ways of life, Merton shows how the tensions among them open into deeper truth.

My reflections on these matters, though rooted in Merton, grow out of my own thinking as well. I hope I have not contradicted anything the monk might have said. But if I have, may paradox abound!

The Way of Marxism

Merton's interest in Marxism probably had several sources. He entered the monastery in a mood of world rejection, but he soon learned to love the world. That love led him to stay informed about what made the world tick, and in Merton's time, Marxism was a key part of the clockwork. The fact that many Christians regard Marx as the Antichrist no doubt appealed to the contrarian in Merton, who loved to explore "the other side" of everything, especially if it might puncture Christian piosity. And surely Merton was attracted by the fact that contradiction was at the heart of Marx's own life and thought, as Merton points out in a passage that reveals the monk as much as Marx:

> Karl Marx would not work for his living, or even write for money. Yet he got Engels to write articles for him, which he sold to the New York *Tribune*. Engels practically supported Marx in England: Engels, who was one of the bosses in his father's capitalist firm in Manchester. Out of these contradictions springs the genial theory of alienation, and the humanism of labor. . . . Shall we on this account disbelieve everything he said? No, for he was a

great diagnostician. He saw the disease of modern man, who has come to be ruled by things and by money, and by machines. . . . In any case, there is no point in judging the inner contradictions of Marx's life with an exaggerated severity. All men, especially all who have talent, tend to be inconsistent. Their very struggle with their inconsistency seeks an outlet and a solution in creative works. But what is significant in Marx is that his analysis of society is a keenly intuitive analysis of inconsistency. He is quick to see the hidden contradictions in every ideology, every social structure.[5]

According to Marx (who borrowed from Hegel), contradiction is the engine of history, the source of historical movement. This process, called the dialectic, moves through three stages. At any given moment, history is dominated by a "thesis," or a dominant state of affairs. But sooner or later, opposition develops to that thesis, an opposition called the "antithesis." Out of that tension, a new and higher state called a "synthesis" will emerge. But then the synthesis becomes a thesis, a new contradiction sets in, and the dialectical drama continues.

Marx believed that the dialectic always develops around economic factors, that economic factors are the only real forces shaping and changing human life. The contradictions that move history arise from the different, and unequal, relations people have to the center of economic power and privilege. In the modern era, under capitalism, the basic contradiction is easily described: a very few people are owners who control economic power, while the vast majority are workers who are controlled by it. Many men and women are exploited through hard work and low pay so that a few may grow overly rich through no effort or virtue of their own. Marx believed that this contradiction would eventually become a conflict, with workers rising up against the owners in a great revolution. The outcome of this collision of thesis and antithesis would be a new synthesis, the classless society, in which economic injustice is eradicated as each gives according to ability and each takes according to need.

Marx minced no words when he named the role of religion in all this: "Religion is the opiate of the people." Religion, Marx argued, serves merely to justify economic injustice, to rationalize the difference between the haves and the have-nots. Rich people believe that God has blessed them for their merits and that the poor deserve their plight. Poor people believe that God has promised them a better life beyond this world, "pie in the sky when you die by-and-by." As Marx saw it, religion possesses no power for change toward justice, only the power to drug people into acceptance of an unjust status quo.

On the face of it, Marxism and Christianity seem to be as contrary as two belief systems can be. But contradictions tend to travel away from each other on great circles that come together again. Merton saw that Marxism and Christianity, though originating in very different assumptions about the nature of reality, come full circle in certain respects. Despite the fact that Marxism denies the reality and power of the Spirit, it reminds us of dimensions of Christianity that Christians have a bad habit of forgetting.

For example, Marxism and Christianity converge in the idea that "religion is the opiate of the people," if by religion we mean its intellectual and institutional forms. Jesus, the prophets, and many mystics tried to give voice to the living experience of God against the dead forms of their times, and Bonhoeffer advocated "religionless Christianity." The hope of every authentic religious leader is to break people's addiction to dead forms of faith and lead them to dependence on the living God. So Marx's critique of religion in its institutional and intellectual forms is the stock in trade of every religious virtuoso.

Marxism and Christianity also converge in their shared concern for the plight of the poor. Of course, that claim cannot be sustained by looking at the affluent mainstream of American religious life. Here is a classic illustration of how religion has become a drug to dull consciousness, extinguishing the passion for the poor that burned at the heart of Jesus' ministry. In this sense, Marx was right: we use religion to justify ourselves, and the religion of many middle-class Americans is designed to allow them to live complacently in the midst of glaring economic injustice.

But if we return to the source and read the New Testament with a clear eye, we see that economic justice and salvation are inextricably linked: "Blessed are you poor, for yours is the Kingdom of God" (Luke 6:20); "it is easier for a camel to go through the eye of a needle than for a rich man to enter the

Kingdom of God" (Matthew 19:24). If these are not the most oft-quoted passages of scripture on Sunday morning, it is not because they lack centrality in Jesus' view of things.

A third convergence between Marxism and Christianity is in the idea of the classless society. A passage in Acts describes the church of Pentecost as a community in which each gave according to ability and took according to need: "And all who believed were together and had all things in common; and they sold their possessions and goods and distributed them all, as any had need" (Acts 2:44–45). In early Christian understanding, the church is intended as a harbinger of things to come, of a world in which all will care for all. So there is a profound parallel between Marxist and Christian *hope*, one pinned on the classless society, the other on an earthly kingdom of God. The eradication of economic injustice is not the only mark of God's kingdom, but it is an essential one.

A fourth convergence between Marxism and Christianity undergirds the other three: both assert that we are enslaved by a "false consciousness," a false understanding of our origins and destiny. And both aim at shattering that false consciousness so that we may know the truth, and the truth can set us free. Marx decried our bondage to economic powers and proclaimed revolutionary class struggle as the road to liberation. Jesus decried our bondage to sin—not least its economic form—and proclaimed that liberation would come as we submitted to God's justice, mercy, and love. There are substantial differences between these diagnoses, of course, but in the midst of contradiction, there is a common theme: Marxism and Christianity alike want to shatter our illusions, reveal our true condition, and empower us to act in ways that will win our liberation.

By allowing Christianity and Marxism to create their own dialectic, Merton was able to develop a critical perspective on monastic life—a perspective premised on principles within the Christian tradition that Marxism helped Merton reclaim. Such is the power of paradox: apparently alien points of view can remind us of the inner truth of our own! I want to explore Merton's critique of monasticism here because it applies to all of us on spiritual paths, whether we are monks or not.

The challenge Merton drew from Marxism and put to the monks can be summed up in two words: "Justify yourself!"— words that are themselves paradoxical if you believe, as Merton did, that we are justified by grace alone. In one of his talks to the novices, Merton reminds the would-be monks that every time they take a bite of food, they depend on the labor of others for their very existence.[6] Even the monk who has "left the world" is not really out of the world—as long as he has to eat, he is beholden to the world's labor. The question is, how do we make sure that our dependencies are not one-sided and exploitative? How do we live in fair exchange so that what we consume is balanced out by what we produce? How can our spiritual labors be as useful to the people who feed us as their labors are to us?

These questions may annoy people who believe that our spiritual life, our relation to God, is an end in itself and thus needs no external justification. That is true, but only as one pole of a paradox! For it is equally true that "you will know them by their fruits" (Matthew 7:20). The challenge to make our spiritual journeys fruitful seems especially important today when so much that passes for spirituality is narcissistic, self-obsessed, and self-indulgent. What are the fruits of your spiritual life—and mine?

Merton's response to this question reveals his capacity to transcend thesis and antithesis. If he were to justify monastic life in a Marxist mode, Merton would have to exhort the monks to produce useful material goods. But Merton, who often carped at the monastery's moneymaking enterprises ("More cheeses for Jesus!" was one of his favorite jabs), does not go that route. Instead he argues that the monastery must repay its debt to the world's labor by "producing people," an obligation that surely applies to every form of spiritual pursuit.

And what does it mean to "produce people"? For Merton, the answer is simple: it means developing the capacity to love, which in turn means doing the hard work of reclaiming and deepening that capacity. Merton makes his point to the novices by using the image of the heart:

> If I love God, I've got to love him with my heart. If I love him with my heart, I've got to have a heart, and I've got to have it in my possession to give. One of the most difficult things in life today is to gain possession of one's heart in order to be able to give it. We don't have a heart to give. We have been deprived of these things, and the first step in the spiritual life is to get back what we have to give.[7]

Here Merton reveals, implicitly, a deep and vital convergence of Marxism and Christianity. Where Marx spoke of the alienation of labor, Merton speaks of the alienation of our hearts. Where Marx argued that capitalism robbed people of both the meaning and the benefits of their work, Merton argues that modern life robs us of our hearts. Here is how Merton put it in his final talk, just an hour or two before he died:

> The idea of alienation is basically Marxist, and what it means is that man living under certain economic conditions is no longer in possession of the fruits of his life. His life is not his. It is lived according to conditions determined by somebody else. I would say that on this particular point, which is very important indeed in the early Marx, you have a basically Christian idea. Christianity is against alienation. Christianity revolts against the alienated life. The whole New Testament is, in fact—and can be read by a Marxist-oriented mind as—a protest against religious alienation.[8]

What does it mean to be robbed of our hearts? For one thing, it means that our ability to feel connected with others and implicated in their lives has been stolen from us, for it is through our hearts that we feel solidarity with our brothers and sisters. It is a common malady in modern times, this inability to empathize with the stranger.

Whatever Karl Marx's failings may have been, he had deep empathy for the plight of the poor, the kind of empathy Jesus called for when he said, "As you did it to one of the least of these my brethren, you did it to me" (Matthew 25:40). But the conditions of modern life have callused many hearts. We seem unable to have our hearts broken by the fact that millions of children are starving and millions of parents are powerless to provide. Our individualized way of life makes us feel alone and unrelated, and our competitive way of life justifies our gains coming at other people's expense.

Merton is right: we don't have possession of our hearts. They have been taken from us by the drive to self-preservation and self-enhancement and by the power of institutions that serve these ends. If we are to give our hearts, we must get them back, and that is the first task in the spiritual life. How strange that Marxism, which seems heartless to so many Christians, would remind Merton that we must regain our hearts! Such is the nature of contradiction as it deepens into paradox.

But to be in possession of our hearts is not simply to be able to feel. Since the heart is an image for our whole being, we must also be able to translate feelings into action, to work on behalf of the Beloved Community. And here is where Merton and the Christian tradition diverge again from Marx, who relied on violence to overthrow the powers that be. Marx believed that the contradictions of history led inevitably to violence and that the classless society would only be hastened when the oppressed declared war against the oppressors.

There is another theory of social change that faces the contradictions of history as squarely as Marx did but proposes a very different course of action. The theory of nonviolence is premised on the notion that beyond every conflict lies a resolution, a synthesis, a common good that will be lost through violence but can be brought into being by patience, dialogue, and prayer. Since the contending parties are usually in no mood for prayer, it is the work of the nonviolent mediator to stand between the antagonists and, by attitudes and actions, serve as a living guide to life-giving change. The mediator quite literally "lives the contradiction."

Thomas Merton was committed to nonviolence, and I want to explore one of its major sources in his life. Doing so will reveal yet another of the multiple and overlapping paradoxes that shaped Merton's thought. From "heartless" Marxism, which was one of the major theories of social action in Merton's time, Merton drew lessons not about action but about the affairs of the heart. For an understanding of right action, Merton drew on Taoism, one of the ancient religions of China, which is widely (and wrongly) understood to advocate retreat from the world and passive acceptance of what is given. In Merton's thought, paradox knows no end!

The Way of Chuang Tzu

Wu wei is the Chinese word for "nonaction," and it occurs often in *The Way of Chuang Tzu*, a Taoist classic that Merton loved and helped translate into English. It is not a word with which the Western mind would launch an exploration of social action, but there it is, a paradox in all its glory! A poem from Chuang Tzu—a Taoist master who lived four centuries before the common era—gives some sense of how *wu wei* is used in that tradition:

Fishes are born in water,

Man is born in Tao.

If fishes, born in water,

Seek the deep shadow

Of pond and pool,

All their needs

Are satisfied.

If man, born in Tao,

Sinks into the deep shadow

Of non-action (*wu wei*)

To forget aggression and concern,

He lacks nothing

His life is secure.

Moral: "All the fish needs

Is to get lost in water.

All man needs is to get lost

in Tao."[9]

On the face of it, the poem seems to counsel a return to the womb, a withdrawal from the problems and pressures of society for the sake of personal happiness. It sounds like narcissism and seems to contradict the Marxist impulse toward social engagement. If we are to see how this contradiction becomes a paradox, and thus understand why Merton was so deeply drawn to the religious experience of the East, we must first understand Merton's critique of social action as it is commonly defined and practiced.

Merton became the patron saint of social activists because he spoke so clearly to their condition. He understood what it means to be driven by the desire to hasten the coming of the Beloved Community:

> Douglas Steere remarks very perceptively that there is a pervasive form of contemporary violence to which the idealist fighting for peace by nonviolent methods most easily succumbs: activism and overwork. The rush and pressure of modern life are a form, perhaps the most common form, of its innate violence. To allow oneself to be carried away by a multitude of conflicting concerns, to surrender to too many demands, to commit oneself to too many projects, to want to help everyone in everything is to succumb to violence. More than that, it is cooperation in violence. The frenzy of the activist neutralizes his work for peace. It destroys his own inner capacity for peace. It destroys the fruitfulness of his own work, because it kills the root of inner wisdom which makes work fruitful.[10]

Note that Merton is troubled not solely by the cost of activism to the activist. He is also concerned about the cost society pays for a type of social action that turns out to be violence in disguise. In his essay "Contemplation in a World of Action," he makes this clear:

> He who attempts to act and do things for others or for the world without deepening his own self-understanding, freedom, integrity and capacity to love, will not have anything to give others. He will communicate to them nothing but the contagion of his own obsessions, his aggressiveness, his ego-centered ambitions, his delusions about ends and means, his doctrinaire prejudices and ideas. There is nothing more tragic in the modern world than the misuse of power and action to which men are driven by their own Faustian misunderstandings and misapprehensions.[11]

Those "Faustian misunderstandings and misapprehensions" are the core of the problem, and Taoism aims at rooting them out. Social action requires power, but whenever we humans come close to power, trouble follows. We think we want power as a means to other ends, but holding power tends to become an end in itself. We think we want power to work for the common good but are tempted to use it for purposes of self-promotion and self-enhancement. Not only do these tendencies deflect our action from its original aims, but they also often lead to acts that are simply counterproductive. Taoism serves to criticize and clarify our action, showing up our conception of power for the delusion it is and guiding us toward a right relation with true power. Only by moving with Tao—the Way, the nonviolent will of God—can we hope to bring peace on earth.

The way in which our illusions about power defeat our best-intended actions is illustrated by Chuang Tzu's poem "The Need to Win":

When an archer is shooting for nothing

He has all his skill.

If he shoots for a brass buckle

He is already nervous.

If he shoots for a prize of gold

He goes blind

Or sees two targets—

He is out of his mind!

His skill has not changed. But the prize

Divides him. He cares.

He thinks more of winning

Than of shooting—

And the need to win

Drains him of power.[12]

The poem does not counsel against winning—it is a paradoxical counsel on how to win! It says that the only way to achieve victory is to forget about victory. When Taoism tells us not to care, it does not mean that we should be indifferent to the many needs around us but rather that we should not let our desire to meet these needs drain us of the power to do so. Every thoughtful activist knows how the desire for success and the fear of failure can pervert our action and even lead to fraud, causing us to settle for the *appearance* of victory rather than persisting for deep and lasting change. When we are trapped in the dualism of winning and losing, we are possessed by false powers.

The paradox that we can win only by forgetting about winning is Christianity 101, I think. It anticipates (by four centuries) Jesus' counsel that if we seek life, we will lose it, but if we lose life in God, we will find it. Taoism pushes us even further by insisting that our actions must transcend not only the polarity of winning and losing but the polarity of good and evil as well.

Here Western sensibilities tend to be offended. Here we want to say that this paradox business has gone far enough! For surely if there is any motive force for right action or any plumb line against which our actions can be judged, it is in ethics, in the distinction between right and wrong. What D. T. Suzuki writes about the Christian reaction to Zen can also be said of our response to Taoism:

> The Zen-man . . . who talks of going beyond the dualism of good and evil, of right and wrong, of life and death, of truth

and falsehood, will most likely be a subject of suspicion. The idea of social values deeply ingrained in Western minds is intimately connected with religion so that they are led to think religion and ethics are one and the same, and that religion can ill-afford to relegate ethics to a position of secondary importance.[13]

But religion is not the same as ethics. In fact, it can be argued that ethics arise as religion declines.

Taoism reminds us that true religion is a mode of connectedness with the hidden wholeness of life. When we are connected, our actions are most likely to be responsive to the needs of the whole. Only when we lose our connection with one another do we need a code of conduct to tell us what we ought to do. When life becomes fragmented, our organic responsiveness to one another is replaced by "oughts." Eventually these oughts become a system of abstract thought far removed from human need, a creed to be defended rather than a relationship to be lived.

Life beyond ethics is no libertine life, no denial of moral discipline. On the contrary, to live a life of true connectedness is a spiritual discipline of the highest order, a source of right action and true power. John Middleton Murry said it well, I think: "For the good man to realize that it is better to be whole than to be good is to enter on a strait and narrow path compared to which his previous rectitude was flowery license."[14]

A number of Chuang Tzu's poems portray the "well-connected" life, the life through which the Tao flows unimpeded into creative activity. One of my favorites is "The Woodcarver":

Khing, the master carver, made a bell stand
Of precious wood. When it was finished,
All who saw it were astounded. They said it must be
The work of spirits.
The Prince of Lu said to the master carver:
"What is your secret?"

Khing replied: "I am only a workman:
I have no secret. There is only this:
When I began to think about the work you commanded
I guarded my spirit, did not expend it
On trifles, that were not to the point.
I fasted in order to set
My heart at rest.
After three days fasting,
I had forgotten gain and success.
After five days
I had forgotten praise or criticism.
After seven days
I had forgotten my body
With all its limbs.

"By this time all thoughts of your Highness
And of the court had faded away.
All that might distract me from the work
Had vanished.
I was collected in the single thought
Of the bell stand.

"Then I went to the forest
To see the trees in their own natural state.
When the right tree appeared before my eyes,
The bell stand also appeared in it, clearly, beyond doubt.
All I had to do was to put forth my hand
And begin.

"If I had not met this particular tree
There would have been
No bell stand at all.

"What happened?
My own collected thought
Encountered the hidden potential in the wood;
From this live encounter came the work
Which you ascribe to the spirits."[15]

For me, this poem has endlessly rich implications for action. Let me draw out only a few. First, the woodcarver, as Merton comments, "does not simply proceed according to certain fixed rules and external standards."[16] In our age, an age dominated by method and technique, this comes near to being heresy! But deep down, we know that mastery in any realm goes beyond rules and methods, just as truly responsive action goes beyond codes of conduct. Ultimately, an artist follows not rules but the spirit, the internal flow, the nature of the thing at hand. This is the way of greatness whether we are speaking of woodcarving, music, or human relationships: it is based on a deep mutuality between the actor and the other, not on an operating manual.

Second, the mutuality that right action requires does not, paradoxically, "come naturally" to us. It can be achieved only through discipline. It is no accident that the woodcarver fasted before beginning his work: let fasting stand for all those disciplines by which we attain (in Merton's words) "detachment, forgetfulness of results, and abandonment of all hope of profit."[17] Only by such means can we transcend those anxieties about self and success that distort work in the world. Only by such means can we discern the intrinsic nature of the problem, the thing, or the person to which our action relates.

Third, action woodcarver-style requires a belief that all things and all people have a "nature," which is to say limits and potentials. This belief is alien to us in the modern

Western world. Our culture insists that all things from trees to people are infinitely malleable and can be changed into whatever shape we want them to take. Today, a bell stand would be made from whatever tree is most cost-effective and mass-produced by machine. And if we want to change our human shape, physical or psychological or spiritual, there are technologies that promise to do so. Most contemporary social action is based on this assumption, I think: that people can be transformed into whatever shape fits the activist's conception of how things "ought" to be. Witness the activism that led to our ill-begotten war in Vietnam.

The woodcarver's message is clearly different. Here true action, action that is full of grace and beauty and authentic results, is based on discernment of and respect for the nature of the other. The reason is simple: only through such a relationship to the rest of reality can our action flow with the action of the Tao. Only so can we become channels for real power.

Oh, we can make bell stands any way we wish. We can hack and hew our way through forests with no regard for the nature of the wood. We can produce a stand that will hold a bell without bothering about the Tao. But we do so at great cost to the world and to ourselves. Not only do we endanger our own survival when we misuse and abuse the forests, but we also deprive our lives of quality. So it is with much of our social action, action that does not respect the nature of the other, action that depends exclusively on human power and is perverted by human pride. Through Taoism, Merton learned another image of action. It is one we need to know in our own strained, frenzied, and violent times.

Although Taoism stands on premises quite different from Merton's Christianity and seems to contradict Christian tradition at key points (as in its devaluation of ethics), the more deeply we pursue the contradictions, the clearer the paradox becomes. For the Taoist image of action has much in common with images in the New Testament. The idea that success is achieved by not worrying about success coheres with the notion that we find our lives by losing them. The idea that we should act without fear of the consequences finds its counterpart in the counsel "do not be anxious about tomorrow" (Matthew 6:34). And the notion that we must empty ourselves to serve as channels for the Tao is echoed in the life of one who renounced all worldly power—who "emptied himself" and "became obedient unto death, even death on a cross" (Philippians 2:7, 8)—so that God's power could be shown through him.

But still the contradiction persists, and the mention of the cross reminds us why. The man or woman of Tao is always portrayed as the invisible person, the person who attracts no attention and encounters no opposition. In the words of one poem:

If you can empty your own boat

Crossing the river of the world,

No one will oppose you,

No one will seek to harm you.[18]

And yet in Christian tradition, the person who incarnates God's truth ends up on the cross. Opposition, harm, and betrayal are, in the Christian view, potential consequences of "speaking truth to power"—another contradiction, and one that was pivotal to Merton's life. For wherever Merton's thought took him—through Marxism, Taoism, and anywhere else—the cross remained his central symbol and reality.

The Way of the Cross

The cross is, first of all, a historical fact. As such, it reminds us of one of history's major contradictions. Throughout the human story, men and women have yearned for truth and goodness to touch their lives. But when truth and goodness appear among us in human form, we are sometimes so threatened that we kill the one who fulfills our wish.

The cross is also a symbol of contradictions whose very structure suggests the oppositions of life. As its crossbar reaches left and right, the cross represents the way we are pulled between conflicting demands and obligations on life's "horizontal" plane. As its vertical member reaches up and down, the cross represents the way we are stretched in that dimension of life, pulled between heaven and earth. To walk the way of the cross is to be torn by opposition and contradiction, tension and conflict.

And yet the way of the cross is also a path toward peace, symbolized by that central place where the arms of the cross converge. For Christians, the cross speaks of the greatest paradox of all: that to live, we have to die. To walk the way of the cross, to allow one's life to be torn by contradiction and swallowed up in paradox, is to live in the hope of resurrection, in the sign of Jonah. For Christians, the crossing point is a place of transformation.

The insights Merton gained from the ways of Marx and Chuang Tzu were, it seems to me, transformed by the way of the cross. From his encounters with Marxism, Merton drew the paradoxical reminder that Christians must regain their alienated hearts in order to give them. For all its materialism and atheism, Marxism begins in profound empathy for the wretched of the earth, a sensibility that has largely been lost in affluent Christian circles. We are afraid to recover our hearts, afraid that we will feel too much and be overwhelmed with pain. We may talk a good line about Jesus, but we fear his example, that "man of sorrows, and acquainted with grief" (Isaiah 53:3).

The problem with Marxism is not that it fails to feel pain but that it has no way to transform pain into a life-giving force. Instead, Marxism allows pain to pursue its natural course toward anger, violence, and more pain. Suffering, unmediated and unalloyed, has only one outcome: more suffering. It may multiply within the person who suffers, or that person may pass it on to others in a futile attempt to find relief. The natural economy of suffering requires a continual inflation of the currency.

Marx's prescription for a suffering society calls for violent revolution followed by a "dictatorship" of the working class. Somehow, these steps are supposed to lead to a society of equity and peace. But we know that the pain will only persist. We have no reason to believe that change by violence and dictatorship foreshadows anything other than violence and dictatorship. At best, the Marxist revolution might cause oppressor and oppressed to switch roles, and there would be grim justice in that. But Marxism offers no way to transform pain into peace.

In contrast, the cross says, "The pain stops here." The way of the cross is a way of absorbing pain, not passing it on, a way that transforms pain from destructive impulse into creative power. When Jesus accepted the cross, his death opened up a channel for the redeeming power of love. When we accept the crosses and contradictions in our lives, we allow that same power to flow. When we give our hearts to the world, our hearts will be broken—broken open to become channels for a love greater than our own. Only as pain is transformed by love will the real revolution come, a revolution that promises to take us toward the "peaceable kingdom."

The way of the cross is often misunderstood as masochistic, especially in an age so desperately in search of pleasure. But the suffering of which Jesus spoke is not the suffering that unwell people create for themselves. Instead, it is the suffering already present in the world, which we can either identify with or ignore. If pain were not real, if it were not the lot of so many, the way of the cross would be pathological. But in our world— with its millions of hungry, homeless, and hopeless people—it is pathological to live as if pain did not exist. The way of the cross means allowing that pain to carve one's life into a channel through which the healing stream of the spirit can flow to a world in need.

The image of a stream recalls Taoism, "the watercourse way," whose aim is the same as Christianity: to bring our words, actions, and beings into the flow of a power that is beyond all names. But Taoism seems to say that once we enter that stream, we float along in ease, while Christianity insists that the stream is full of obstacles and whitewater and danger, that the flow of the spirit will bring us to the cross.

But Christians also believe that the stream of spirit will take us beyond the cross, that the way of the cross is ultimately a way of joy. If Jesus was "a man of sorrows, and acquainted with grief," he was also the one who said, "My yoke is easy, and my burden is light" (Matthew 11:30). What we lose on the cross is not our lives but our burden of falsehood and illusion; what lives beyond the cross is the uplifting power of love. The paradox of the crucifixion is the death of the illusion that death is supreme; the paradox of our own crossing points is that pain kills illusion so truth can bring joy.

The way of the cross reminds us that despair and disillusionment are not dead ends but signs of impending resurrection.

Losing our illusions is painful because illusions are the stuff we live by. But God is the great iconoclast, constantly smashing the idols on which we depend. Beyond illusion lies a fuller truth that can be glimpsed only as our falsehoods die. As we have the faith to live fully in the midst of these painful contradictions, we will experience resurrection and the transformation of our lives.

Thomas Merton spoke often of two illusions that must die on the cross if we are to become channels of the Spirit. The first is the "false self," a self that separates us from God and from each other. This is the self full of pride and pretense, the self that tries to control life for its own benefit. This is the self that wants to resolve all contradictions by ignoring or denying them, the self that hopes to live without ambiguity or pain. This is the idolatrous self, the self that thinks it is God and wants to create the world in its own image. This false self must die if we are to live—but since it is for a long time the only self we know, we struggle to keep it alive and lose it only when we are overwhelmed by pain.

Here, as everywhere, there is a paradox! In order to lose one's ego, one must have an ego to lose. There seems to be a need for each person to build up a false sense of self, of difference from others, before the spiritual struggle to become part of the "hidden wholeness" can begin. Deeper still, there is the paradox that not until the false self dies does the true self come into being. The destruction of ego does not mean a loss of personhood. The individual in whom the false self has been shattered is not a faceless cipher or a pale imitation of the real thing. Instead, this is a person in whom flow all the currents of life, human and divine.

The second illusion that must die on the cross is our false conception of the world. The two illusions are related, since much of the false self is built around our notion of what "the world" wants and demands of us. Merton was especially sensitive to our images of the world because he saw the monasteries attracting men motivated by world rejection. He fought hard against this temptation to see the world as evil and the spiritual life as pure, insisting instead that we live into the contradictions and discover the underlying paradox.

In one of his talks to the novices, Merton chides them for thinking of the world as an independent entity, a thing "out there," capable of imposing demands and conditions on their lives.[19] It is wrong, he says, to come to the monastery in order to escape the world so conceived, for the conception is false. The world, Merton insists, does not begin at the monastery gatehouse: it is *within* each one of us. The world will be a force "out there" constraining and diverting our energies only if we grant that illusion reality and let it govern our lives.

Again, the pain of living the contradictions is partly the pain of having our illusions shattered. We construct the illusion of a powerful world "out there" because it lets us off the hook: "The world made me do it." When the contradictions of life show us how *internal* that world really is, we are loath to give up our excuse. It is more comforting to believe that the world is an external power that compels us than to accept the fact that we have the freedom to respond fully to God's will.

After all is said and done, freedom is what the cross is all about. After the tension, after the suffering, after the death, after the resurrection comes freedom. As Merton once observed, "The cross is . . . the only liberation from . . . servitude to the illusions which are packaged and sold as 'the world.'"[20] The cross liberates us from the idea that the world is "out there," over and against us; the experience of the cross reveals that the world is in us, in both its glory and its shame.

So we can see the truth in Merton's words that "the world is a matter of interpenetration and is not something absolute like a brick structure. The world isn't something we have to adjust to. It's something we adjust."[21] Since the world is in us, we are responsible for the world—and the shape the world takes depends on how we live our lives. The cross brings freedom, and with that freedom comes responsibility, "the ability to respond" to the claims of justice.

The liberation of the cross goes further still. Not only are we freed from illusion and freed to respond, but we are also freed in the knowledge that the world is redeemed by a God who suffers contradictions with us. As long as we see the world as unredeemed, we will want to redeem it ourselves. The consequences of that impossible expectation are well known—frustration, anger, impotence, guilt, and despair. But in the light of the cross, we can see the world and ourselves in a new way. For God is already at work here, suffering brokenness but always offering the gift of reconciliation. By accepting the cross in our own lives, we will be brought into the stream of sacred work and given the gift of hope.

So in the manner of paradox, we come full circle. By living the contradictions, we will come to hope, and in hope will we be empowered to live life's contradictions. How do we break into this circle that goes round and round with no apparent point of entry? Someday, far out at sea, heading away from the place where God has called us, lost in contradictions, we will be swallowed by grace and find ourselves—with Jonah, with Merton, with all the saints—traveling toward our destiny in the belly of a paradox.

CHAPTER II

The Stations of the Cross

Among Catholic Christians, there is an ancient tradition involving the "stations of the cross," each station corresponding to a key point in Jesus' journey to his crucifixion. You can find these stations portrayed in carved wood or stained glass along the passageways of parish churches. Here the faithful walk, pause, and pray, remembering Christ's sacrifice, opening themselves to the special insight that each station represents. There is the point at which Jesus falls, the one at which Simon of Cyrene carries the cross for Jesus, the one at which Jesus meets his mother, the one at which Jesus is nailed to the cross. Each point is full of portent and power for those who have eyes to see and ears to hear.

It seems to me there is another series of stations of the cross, stations that represent not steps of an outward journey but moments of an inner movement as we live our lives through death toward resurrection. I want to write about five such moments that come from my inward experience: I call them recognition, resistance, acceptance, affirmation, and liberation.

Of course, this inward way of the cross does not always proceed in that order. And once we have passed through the five stations, the journey is not over: it will recur again and again. This process goes on in our lives whether we acknowledge it or not, and talking about it will neither prevent it nor make it easier. But by speaking of these inner stations of the cross, we can grow in awareness of the path we are on, learn what we need to learn, and grow in faith and hope about the journey's destination.

Recognition

First, recognition. The cross calls us to recognize that the heart of the human experience is neither consistency nor chaos but contradiction. In the twentieth century, we were beguiled by the claim of consistency, by the illusion that history is moving toward the resolution of all problems, by the false hope that comes from groundless optimism. Then when this claim was discredited by tragic events, we were assaulted by theories of chaos, by prophets of despair who claim that everything can be reduced to the random play of forces beyond all control, of events that lack inherent meaning.

But the cross symbolizes that beyond naive hope and beyond meaningless despair lies a structure of dynamic contradictions in which our lives are caught. The cross represents the way in which the world contradicts God: we yearn for light and truth and goodness to appear among us, and yet when they come in human form, the world grows fearful and may kill the incarnation. But then, the cross represents the way in which God contradicts the world: no matter how often the world says no, God is present with an eternal yes, bringing light out of darkness, hope out of despair, life out of death.

The very structure of the cross symbolizes these contradictions. Its arms reach left and right, up and down, signifying the way life pulls us between the conflicting claims of person against person, the conflicting claims of the human and the divine. And yet the arms of the cross converge at the center, symbolizing the way in which God can act in our lives to overcome conflict, to unify the opposition, to contradict the contradictions. The cross calls us to recognize that reality has a cruciform shape.

Loren Eiseley tells a story that helps me feel the power of recognizing and embracing life's contradictions.[1] The great naturalist once spent time in a seaside town called Costabel. Plagued by his lifelong insomnia, Eiseley spent the early morning hours walking the beach. And every day at sunrise, he found townspeople combing the sand for starfish that had washed ashore during the night to kill them for commercial purposes. For Eiseley, it was a sign, however small, of all the ways the world says no to life.

One morning, Eiseley went out unusually early and discovered a solitary figure on the beach. This man, too, was gathering starfish, but each time he found one alive, he would pick it up and throw it as far as he could out beyond the breaking surf, back to the ocean from which it came. Eiseley found this man on his mission of mercy every morning, day after day, no matter the weather.

Eiseley named this man "the star thrower." In a moving meditation, he writes of how this man and his predawn work contradicted everything Eiseley had been taught about evolution and the survival of the fittest. Here on the beach in Costabel, the strong reached down to save, not crush, the weak. And Eiseley wonders, is there a star thrower at work in the universe, a God who contradicts death, whose nature (to quote the words of Thomas Merton) is "mercy within mercy within mercy"?

That story is rich in meaning for me. It offers an image of a God who threw the stars and throws them still. It speaks of how ordinary men and women can participate in God's enveloping mercy. And it suggests a vocation that each of us could undertake on our inward way of the cross: to recognize, identify, and lift up those moments, those acts, those people, those stories that contradict the ways in which the world says no to life.

That is what I mean by calling the first station on this inward way of the cross "recognition." To recognize the cruciform nature of reality is to see that the world is not monolithic, that things are not locked in place, that God is always moving among and within us, contradicting the trend of antilife no matter how strong that trend may be. These contradictions may be few in number, but that does not matter. They become transforming when we recognize their superior reality and live in a way that makes that reality manifest and abundant. The world is full of hate. But once you have been loved, you can live in the power of that moment and make it multiply.

I like to think of Christians as star throwers. I like to think of all those, Christians or not, who have stood at the shoreline of history, have stood against the surf and the tide, and forgetting all fear of looking foolish, have reached down to affirm life no matter how small and insignificant its form. How fragile is the commitment to peace against the incessant evolution of war. And yet by standing in that foolish place, we contradict the course of social evolution. By living the contradiction, we participate in the power and hope of the cross.

One way of naming that power and hope comes from the poet Rainer Maria Rilke in his classic *Letters to a Young Poet*. He wrote not about the cross but about the importance of "living the questions." But if you replace *questions* with *contradictions*, as I have done here, Rilke helps us understand the dynamics of embracing a cruciform way of life:

> Be patient toward all that is unresolved in your heart. . . .
> Try to love the contradictions themselves. . . . Do not now
> seek the resolutions, which cannot be given because you

would not be able to live them, and the point is to live everything. Live the contradictions now. Perhaps you will then gradually, without noticing it, live along some distant day into the resolutions.[2]

Resistance

The second station on this inward way of the cross is resistance. It is not easy to be a star thrower, to stand against the tides. There is much in our human nature that resists living the contradictions, that wants to avoid the tension that comes from being torn between the poles. But because reality has a cruciform shape, avoidance is futile. For example, I abhor war, but I continue to pay war taxes, trying to avoid getting crosswise with the powers that be. But in that evasion, I am caught in yet another tension, impaled on yet another cross, torn between my own convictions and my inability to act them out.

I have come to believe that our resistance to such crosses—indeed, our resistance to God's will—is not a moral failing but another aspect of the cruciform nature of reality. If we can recognize it as such, our resistance can generate energy for life. By neither denying nor ignoring those tensions but living consciously in them, we stand a greater chance of being pulled open to the power of the Spirit.

I see this power illustrated in scripture, especially the Hebrew Bible. Those texts are full of stories of people resisting God, arguing with God, trying to trick and outwit God, flying in the face of God's commands. I like all of that because it humanizes the spiritual life, portraying God as willing and able to enter the human fray. How often in our Christian piety do we treat God as an abstract principle who cannot enter the realities of the flesh? Come to think about it, that is rank heresy! By turning earthy Hebraic holiness into a philosophical Greek abstraction, we deprive ourselves of a great source of energy for life, a dynamic relationship with a God we can wrestle with as Jacob wrestled with the angel.

I believe that it is God's will that I devote my whole self to the establishment of peace on earth. But how I struggle against that will! How I try to bargain with God, arguing that other claims on my life must be honored too: the claims of family, of career, of limited time and energy, of my prudent fears about the consequences of responding too fully to what is asked of me.

But as I live in that resistance—as I acknowledge and confess it to myself and others—slowly my life is pulled open. In the tension created within me by my fear of confronting war taxes, I am opened to other ways I might witness for peace. I look within my family and find ways of living in harmony. I look at my career and find ways of using my gifts toward building the Beloved Community. My resistance itself, my argument with God about what I *cannot* do, stretches me to discover what I *can* do to witness to the light.

There is another important reason to trust our resistance to the cross: some crosses are false, not given by God. They are laid upon us by a heedless world and embraced by an unhealthy part of ourselves. Christian tradition has too many examples of masochism masquerading as the way of the cross. And the church is full of people who submit too easily to injustices that ought to be fought. So we have the problem of distinguishing valid crosses from invalid ones, crosses that lead toward the crossing point from those that lead to desolation.

I do not know of any abstract principle by which the one can be told from the other. Our embodied resistance is the best test I know. Let us resist any cross that comes our way. Become a pole of opposition. Live the contradiction. As we do so, our false crosses will fall away. But those we must accept, that emerge from reality and not illusion, will stay there right in the middle of our lives, pulling left and right, up and down, until they pull us open to our true center—a center where we are one with God.

Acceptance

First recognition, then resistance, and now the third station on this inward way of the cross: acceptance. Few of us are so spiritually advanced that we can accept the crosses we are given in simple obedience, as a spiritual discipline. So another reason to resist the cross is that by resisting, we become so worn down, so flattened out, so drained of energy and emptied of fight that the only thing left is to accept!

The idea that acceptance follows resistance is confirmed by Elisabeth Kübler-Ross in her study of the stages of dying.[3] She describes how the dying person first goes through denial, then anger, then bargaining, and then depression before finally reaching acceptance. Of course, denial, anger, bargaining, and depression are all forms of resistance; we see them not only in cases of terminal illness but in virtually all our negotiations with life. Only after we have run out of resistance does acceptance come.

This parallel with Kübler-Ross's work is powerful for me because the way of the cross is always a way of dying. On the cross, our false dependencies are revealed. On the cross, our illusions are killed off. On the cross, our small self dies so that the true self, the God-given self, can emerge. On the cross, we give up the fantasy that we are in control, and the death of this fantasy is central to acceptance.

The cross is, above all, a place of powerlessness. Here is the final proof that our own feeble powers can no more alter life's trajectory than a magnet can pull down the moon. Here is the death of the ego, of the self that insists on being in charge, the self that continually tries to impose its own idea of order and righteousness on the world.

But once again, the cross is a place of contradiction. For the powerlessness of the cross, if fully embraced, takes us to a place of power. This is the great mystery at the heart of Christian faith, from Jesus to Martin Luther King Jr., the mystery of the power of powerlessness. Or is it such a mystery after all? As long as I am preoccupied with the marshaling of my own feeble powers, there will be no way for God's power to flow through me. As long as I am getting in my own way, I cannot live in the power of God's way.

Here is how Paul speaks of this moment of acceptance in Jesus' crucifixion and our own: "In your minds you must be the same as Christ Jesus: his state was divine, yet he did not cling to his equality with God but *emptied* himself to assume the condition of a slave, and became as men are; and being as all men are he was humbler yet, even to accepting death, death on a cross" (Philippians 2: 5–7).

"Emptiness" is key in describing the experience of acceptance. Once again I find confirmation in the work of Elisabeth Kübler-Ross, who says that the stage of acceptance in a dying person "should not be mistaken for a happy stage. It is almost void of feelings." Many of us have been in that place, I think, when we have finally accepted a difficult reality and there is simply a hole inside us—not a raw place or a sinking space but a simple emptiness. And so often it is through such emptiness that a larger power can flow through our lives, through the space that has been hollowed out in us by acceptance.

I sometimes have that experience in teaching when I struggle to plan a class but, work as I might, nothing seems right. So I finally give up, yield to my own inability, walk into class feeling empty and afraid—and in that state am somehow able to serve as an open conduit for truth to flow between me and my students. Those are the times the students say how good it was, not the times when I am filled with plans that do not yield to the power of the Spirit!

Jesus on the cross emptied himself so that God might enter. When we accept a cross, a void is created in us, a void that can be filled by the One whose creations begin in nothing. In powerlessness we are given the power of the Spirit.

Affirmation

The fourth station on this inward way of the cross is affirmation. The cross becomes most powerful in our lives when we can go beyond acceptance and say with confidence, hope, and joy: this cross is mine. It is given to me by life, and it is a way to larger life, to community with my brothers and sisters and with God.

The way of the cross may seem a lonely way. But—and here is another contradiction—by walking that lonely way, we find one another. The community we seek will not come because we want it or pursue it. It will come as we are willing to shoulder one another's burdens, pick up one another's crosses, and in the process find ourselves part of a gathered people where "the yoke is easy and the burden is light" because we share it with one another.

It is not easy for us to think of affirming the cross with joy. But I know of no greater joy than the joy of community, of feeling at one, at home with one another. That joy will come only as we are willing to suffer the crossing points that lie at the heart of every relationship. Community means sharing and even creating one another's contradictions. Community means causing each other pain—even the most graced of relationships will someday know the pain of separation. So if we want the joy of community, of relatedness, we must not only accept but also affirm the experience of the cross.

We live in a self-centered time, when the pursuit of self-satisfaction has created too many adults who seem incapable of the vulnerability that authentic relationships require. And long before our time, America's culture of individualism devalued community, blessing only those relationships that served mutual self-interest. The way of the cross cuts through the illusion that such relations bear any resemblance to real life by reminding us that true joy is found on the other side of shared suffering.

When I think about the people with whom I have the deepest sense of community, I think of people who have been able to share with me their contradictions and their brokenness, thus allowing me to share mine. When we present ourselves to the world as smooth and seamless, we allow others no way in, no way to engage in life together. But as we acknowledge and affirm that the cross is the shape of our lives, we open a space within us and between us where community can occur. And in that empty space, in that solitude at the center of the cross, the One who created us whole makes us whole again, giving us cause for joy!

If we are to affirm the true cross and welcome it into our lives, we must understand that at its deepest reaches, the cross is not only a tragic symbol but a comic one as well. The tragic and the comic are constantly crossing paths in the cross, for contradiction is the stuff of which great comedy is made. A comedy builds as you follow the logic of a situation until *zap!* an illogical and unexpected event or remark takes you by surprise. A comic situation is one in which people "get their wires crossed." Until we can see that contradictions are laughable, that the tragic and the comic go hand in hand, we will not be able to affirm the way our lives have been crossed and double-crossed.

Paul refers to the "scandal" of the cross, and in that word we see its comic dimension. A scandal is cause for the snickers and sly grins that reveal our amusement when something happens that contradicts the prevailing order, the conventional scheme of things. The king has no clothing! The mighty have fallen! And that is what the cross is all about. Death is supposed to be the end, so resurrection is a scandal. It makes a person laugh out loud that the powers of death, so arrogant and so certain of themselves, should be defeated on the cross. A scandal of the first order! The ultimate joke!

Liberation

Recognition, resistance, acceptance, affirmation, and finally, the fifth station on this inward way of the cross: liberation. The finest fruit of the cross is liberation, not because freedom is an end in itself but because only as we become free can God use us. Free from our bondage to illusion, our bondage to fear, free ultimately from the confusion of contradictions. On the cross, we are liberated to live in truth, in love, in responsiveness to the movement of the Spirit in our lives. Through the center of the cross, we pass beyond contradiction into the wholeness of life in the Spirit.

The older word for liberation is *salvation*—a difficult word to use these days because it has been so discredited by certain narrow-gauge versions of Christianity. But it is a word we need to reclaim, for its root meaning is "wholeness." To be saved is to be made whole, to be able to enter the unity that lies beyond all of life's contradictions.

Liberation will come only as we experience the cross in our lives: we must suffer the world's no in order to receive the divine yes. Only by allowing life's contradictions to pull us open to the Spirit will we be able to live beyond the dualities that confuse and confound us—the dualities of yes and no, day and night, right and wrong. Life on the way of the cross is, finally, a life of liberty in the Spirit, a life of salvation or wholeness in which contradictions are transcended. The liberation of the cross frees us not for indulgence and ease but for the discipline of serving truth without fearing the contradictions.

To be saved, to be made whole, is to realize that we are in the contradictions and the contradictions are in us and that all of it is held together by a "hidden wholeness." It is to be able to be anywhere with anyone, in freedom and in love. To be whole is to know one's relatedness to all of life, to the dark and the light, the evil and the good, the strange and the familiar. It is to walk freely across the earth knowing that God is with us whether we ascend to the heavens or descend into hell. The liberation of the cross is knowing that there is no contradiction that God cannot overcome.

For those of us who are Christian, it is especially important to understand that the cross liberates us from narrow and confining versions of Christian faith itself. Ultimately, the cross is not about any one faith tradition: it is about the power of God. Thomas Merton, Catholic Christian and Trappist monk, once put this in words that have always seemed quite remarkable to me:

> The Cross is the sign of contradiction—destroying the seriousness of the Law, of the Empire, of the armies. . . . But the magicians keep turning the cross to their own purposes. Yes, it is for them too a sign of contradiction: the awful blasphemy of the religious magician who makes the cross contradict mercy! This is of course the ultimate temptation of Christianity! To say that Christ has locked all the doors, has given one answer, settled everything and departed, leaving all life enclosed in the frightful consistency of a system outside of which there is seriousness and damnation, inside of which there is the intolerable flippancy of the saved—while nowhere is there any place left for the mystery of the freedom of divine mercy which alone is truly serious, and worthy of being taken seriously.[4]

Liberation is frightening, and radical freedom scares us. That is why Erich Fromm wrote about the "escape from freedom" as a characteristic of our totalitarian time.[5] Now Merton identifies the escape from freedom that has imprisoned too many Christian hearts—this tendency to draw tight the boundaries of salvation, to create a system of beliefs and practices that denies the radical freedom of God's mercy to move where it will, within the church and without.

The cross finally contradicts any system of beliefs that tries to capture the cross. The movement of Christ in our lives, our sharing of his cross, liberates us from fear of freedom into freedom from fear. Only then are we fully available to one another, fully available to life, fully available to God.

CHAPTER III

Paradoxes of Community

Parker J. Palmer with Sally Palmer

This essay was written in 1975 during the authors' first year at
Pendle Hill, a Quaker adult study center and living-learning
community near Philadelphia. What began as a yearlong
experiment in community stretched into eleven years in residence. During that time, Parker Palmer served as dean of studies, teacher, and writer in residence, and Sally Palmer served
as a teacher of pottery, weaving, and the spiritual life.

We had talked about community for years. How to create
some "sense of community" where we lived? Whether to
join an existing community—and which one? And what
about the possibility of starting one with some of our
friends? The longer we talked, the more barriers arose
between us and any new way of life. Our family got larger,

we grew older, and as our wants and needs increased our options seemed to narrow.

But the talk created its own pressure, and by February 1974, we knew it was time to put up or shut up. Our dreaming had become a source of frustration, not energy, and an honest look at ourselves revealed that we were beginning to protect life rather than live it.

Why Community?

Our need for community came from feeling isolated and fragmented at work and at home. Sally's concerns revolved around the difficulties of raising three children in suburban seclusion and of forming purposeful relations with other adults amid the logistical chaos of a five-person family. Parker's needs came from the lack of community in academic life and the larger question of civic community in America. Individually and together, we felt a need for community to simplify and integrate the scattered pieces of our lives.

Something had to give! So at the end of a dismal February, the five of us boarded a train and set off for Koinonia Partners in Americus, Georgia, a community we had read about for many years, the community that was to become the birthplace of Habitat for Humanity.[1] We spent only a week there, calendar time, but it was *kairos* time on our spiritual journey. The simple fact of seeing good people living in community, in faithful partnership with the victims of oppression, gave us new hope and direction. And someone down there spoke words that we knew were true but had lacked the courage to say to ourselves: "You don't think your way into a new kind of living; you live your way into a new kind of thinking."

So we returned to Washington committed to spend at least the next year "in community" and with considerable trepidation took our first step: a leave of absence from Parker's job at the university. The prospect of twelve months without paychecks was not comforting, but we knew that community would continue to elude us as long as we put a premium on comfort.

Then began the search for a place. Koinonia Partners was a possibility, and so was another Koinonia near Baltimore. We had read about and corresponded with the Bruderhof.[2] We visited Lindisfarne and Pendle Hill and got in touch with several other groups by phone and letter.[3] These are (or were) very different kinds of places, but they have this much in common: at each of them, a group of people is trying to live together and touch the world, animated by spiritual insight.

We finally chose Pendle Hill, a Quaker living-learning community near Philadelphia, where we took up residence in the fall of 1974. Here we share a daily life of worship, study, physical work, common meals, and recreation with about sixty other people. Their ages range from one to seventy-one. Half or fewer are Quakers, and among the others, several of the world's major religions are represented. Pendle Hill is not a "pure" community. It is also an educational institution with a staff, a board of managers, and a history that dates back to 1930. But at Pendle Hill, we have experienced one of the many versions in which community presents itself, and the experience has been compelling.

Community and Contradiction

If it is true that we live our way into a new kind of thinking, it follows that our ideas about a thing should change with experience. So it has been with our conception of community. We came to community with certain expectations, seeking certain qualities of life. We have found much of what we sought, but we have also found things we neither sought nor thought we wanted. In fact, it sometimes seems that for each thing we sought, we have found not only that thing but also its opposite!

We came seeking a fuller fellowship with others than we had experienced in the suburbs. We found it, but we also discovered a new need for solitude. We came seeking extended family for ourselves and our children. We found it, but we also discovered the need to draw our own family's boundaries more firmly around us. We came seeking to escape certain forces in the world. We have done so, but we have also found ourselves more deeply engaged with the world than ever before.

At first, these polarities were confusing and even demoralizing. We did not understand why life in community so often pulled us between contradictions or impaled us on the horns of dilemmas. But the longer we live in community, the more we realize that these are not contradictions or dilemmas at all. Instead, they have the character of paradox—both poles are true. When either extreme is taken alone, our true needs are not met. But when the poles are held in creative tension with each other, our needs can be met in the round.

Take, for example, our wish for a richer "life together" with others. In the suburbs, we were constantly pulled toward privatism. In fact, it sometimes seems that privacy is the primary product the affluent buy with their wealth. Expensive single-family houses full of mechanical aids, hired household services, costly cars, and elaborate vacation getaways all serve to keep us apart from one another and to deny the underlying truth of our interdependence.

But independence is an unnatural condition for the human species, so just beneath the surface of our privileged privatism lies a cavern of loneliness. We wanted readier access to other people. We wanted life together in a variety of settings—work, play, study, worship—not just on party nights. We wanted more conscious interdependence, of us on others and others on us.

We found such relationships at Pendle Hill, and we celebrate the many ways they have opened and enlarged our lives. But—and here beginneth the paradox—we have also discovered that loneliness can be intensified in community. When we feel lonely, it is much more difficult to be in a community where all around us we can see friendships in which we do not share than to be in a suburb where it seems clear that *everyone* is lonely! When the people at Pendle Hill seem to be a community to each other but only a crowd to us, our loneliness is more piercing than ever.

And now the paradox deepens. For in confronting our own loneliness, we have begun to understand the riches of solitude. Solitude is different from loneliness. Loneliness is a yearning for others that denies the fact that we are, humanly, alone to ourselves. Loneliness is often a refusal to face ourselves; it is rooted in the need to have the faces and voices of others fill up the emptiness we fear within. In solitude, we face into our emptiness and find not a vacuum or a void but an inward space full of light, sweet silence, and perhaps even God.

And from solitude, where we come into deeper possession of ourselves, we can emerge to create true community with others— a community of people who know themselves and can offer themselves to each other, not that colony of psychic parasites that sometimes passes for community. So here is one paradox of community as we have experienced it: our need for solitude and our need for each other, each creating and deepening the other.

Another paradox involves our life as a family. We came to Pendle Hill hoping to broaden and extend our family boundaries. We wanted our children to know adults other than teachers and parents. As parents, we wanted the support of other people in bearing the burdens that can weigh so heavily on the nuclear family.

All of that has happened, and more. Our ten-year-old son can often be found in the kitchen helping one of the young men here bake bread or peel vegetables. When we could not comfort our seven-year-old during his agonies as "the new boy at school," a seventy-year-old woman gave him milk and cookies and autoharp lessons every day after school. Yesterday, our first-grade daughter took a blind woman from the community to school with her, escorting her through the morning's activities completely relaxed about her friend's "otherness."

For us, it has been important simply to see, up close, that our family's problems are not unique and to share solutions—and failures!—with other parents. We have also found that relations within the family are quickened and freshened by the view we get of one another through the eyes of others with whom we interact on a daily basis. And in community, we find that bad family patterns are more easily altered: if a morning squabble occurs, it is less likely to drag on through the day, for we will soon be talking at the communal breakfast with people outside the vicious circle, and soon the spat will be forgotten.

But here is the paradox: in our quest for an extended family of sorts, we have found the need to draw new boundaries around our nuclear family, to identify ourselves more clearly as a group within a group. The richness of association that community provides can also be experienced as a dispersion, a scattering of energies and attentions. We have found it vital to set aside family time and space, to become more conscious of the family circle, lest we begin to feel that we belong to everyone and thus to no one.

Our movement back toward family boundaries may have been motivated at first by fear of loss, but it has become a real affirmation of life together. Because of the community, we are now more aware of what it means to be a family. Community, with its tendency to diffuse family identity, has caused us to reflect more on the value of family life than we ever did when we were a group unto ourselves. And knowing we have a home within a home has freed us to participate even more fully in the larger group's life. So we come to another paradox: the need to extend our family and the need to draw it in, each creating and deepening the other.

Community and the World

A third paradox begins with the fact that we came to community in part to escape certain forces in "the world." We have succeeded to some extent. The pace here is more sane, the scale of things more human, our relations with others less anxious and less competitive, and the pieces of our lives more integrated than before.

But "the world" is very much with us in community. If we have escaped some things, we have also had to engage ourselves and others at a depth to which we are not accustomed. Sometimes it is simply because others are impinging on our rights, or we on theirs, and in community, there is no way to ignore those transgressions. Sometimes it is because community can be a psychic pressure cooker, forcing problems to the surface where they must be dealt with. If dynamics like these are part of what we mean by "the world," then we have not escaped them here. On the contrary, we have been compelled to engage them more deeply.

But the world is more than individuals, their psyches, and their relationships. It is also structures of powers, mass phenomena, the events of history. It is people dying of starvation in Africa and of war in Southeast Asia. Although we continue to weep over our complicity in such evil, and our impotence to do much about it, the deepening paradox of community is that we are beginning to feel more engaged with those dimensions of "the world" as well.

For one thing, community itself seems to be a witness worth making in a society gone mad with competitive individualism and its violent outcomes. As many political theorists have claimed, the recovery of our national political health depends in part on the emergence of more small communities of mutual aid and accountability, the "little platoons" on which Edmund Burke pinned the chances for democracy.[4] For another thing, the community to which we belong is a community of conscience and more: a community that tries to listen for the way God is calling us to respond to the needs of a suffering world.

Life in community makes it more possible to take concrete actions that respond to the claims that God and the world make on our lives. Simple living, for example, is facilitated by community; not only can we share resources, but we can encourage one another in a commitment to consume less. And community offers more support, psychic and otherwise, for the kind of risky action our times require. In sum, that's another paradox of community: in seeking to escape certain forces in the world, we find ourselves more deeply engaged with the condition of our brothers and sisters.

We are not well prepared to understand our lives in terms of paradox. Instead, we have been taught to see and think in dualities: individual versus group, self versus others, contemplative versus active, success versus failure. But the deeper truths of our lives seem to need paradox for full expression. There is truth in both poles, and we live most creatively when we live between them in tension.

Perhaps even more can be said. Perhaps in the synthesis of those apparent opposites, we get closer to truth. Perhaps in living beyond those dualisms, we discover a truth that lies beyond the mind's reach. As William Johnston observed in *Christian Zen*, "It could be argued that Christianity is one tremendous koan that makes the mind boggle and gasp in astonishment; and faith is the breakthrough into that deep realm of the soul which accepts paradox . . . with humility."[5]

Somehow it seems right to us that community is the context in which we have begun to appreciate paradox. Always, in our mind's eye, we have seen community as a circle, and the circle is an image in which the apparent oppositions of life meet, touch, and flow seamlessly into one another. In that circle, we are beginning to get a glimpse of the unity that may lie behind the apparent contradictions of experience.

Although we came to Pendle Hill for just a year, we now plan to stay on for a while, probably three more years, possibly longer. For the time being, at least, community is the context in which we want to live our lives. That could change, and radically: the ultimate paradox may be that an experience in community is incomplete without a season in the hermitage! If that happens, perhaps our understanding of paradox will have deepened enough to sustain us. The aim would be to see life steady and see it whole whether one is in or out of this particular circle—knowing that there are circles within circles within circles, world without end.

CHAPTER IV

A Place Called Community

We expect a theophany of which we know nothing but the
place, and the place is called community.

— MARTIN BUBER, *Between Man and Men*

Surely Buber's words are prophetic. God comes to us in the
midst of human need, and the most pressing needs of our
time demand community in response.

How can I participate in a fairer distribution of resources
unless I live in a community that makes it possible to consume less? How can I learn accountability unless I live in a
community where my acts and their consequences are visible?
How can I learn to share power unless I live in a community
where hierarchy is unnatural? How can I take the risks that
right action demands unless I live in a community that offers
support? How can I learn the sanctity of each life unless I live

in a community where we can be persons, not roles, to one another?

In contrast to these hard questions, the popular image of community is distressingly sentimental. We—especially white, middle-class folk—value community for the personal nurture it promises but ignore its challenges of political and economic justice. We speak of "life together" in romantic terms that bear little resemblance to the difficult discipline of a common life.

But the problems of our age will yield neither to personalism nor to romance. If the idea of community is to speak to our condition, we must change the terms of the discussion. So I write about community partly to correct the romantic fallacy: if we seek a dream community, reality will quickly defeat us, and the struggle for community cannot afford such losses.

I write, too, because the religious basis of community is so often ignored—and I believe that religion points not toward fantasy but toward ultimate reality. The idea of community is at the heart of every great religious tradition. The Hebrew Bible is primarily the narrative of a community making and breaking its covenant with God. The New Testament affirms that the capacity to join with others in a life of prayer and service is one test of receiving God's spirit. Acts of the Apostles, for example, reports that the formation of a community of shared goods was among the first fruits of Pentecost: "All whose faith had drawn them together held everything in common: they would sell their property and possessions and make a general distribution as the need of each required" (Acts 2:44–45).

And from the heart of my own spiritual experience, I know that God is constantly moving within and among us, calling us back to that unity, that wholeness, in which we were created. If we will respond to that call, we can make a critical witness to the possibility of a future both human and divine. In the pages that follow, I shall try to show how and why.

The Quest for Community

Much has been said and written about the quest for community in our time, but the rhetoric is not reflected in our actions. We may honor community with our words, but the history of the twentieth century has been a determined movement away from life together.

For several generations, Americans have been in conscious flight from the extended family and the small town. Both forms of community slowed our progress toward a goal we cherish more deeply than we cherish life together: the goal of economic mobility. Small towns do not offer a wide enough range of jobs to allow us to advance. And if we do get a chance to move on and up, hauling a multigenerational family around with us becomes impossible.

So we have been drawn toward cities large and complex enough to meet our economic desires and families small and portable enough to make mobility possible. Popular sociology portrays us as victims of these "movements" and "trends," as if the woes that accompany modernity had been forced on us. But no. The destruction of intimate community has been at our own hands. It has been a function of our own hierarchy of needs. My point is not that large cities and small families are wrong; clearly, both reflect legitimate values. My point is that those values stand largely in opposition to the value of an all-embracing intimate community. We may yearn for community, but we yearn even more for the social and economic prizes individual mobility can bring.

We can take a first, crucial step away from our romance about community by recognizing that it is a value in conflict with other values we hold—and in our decisions, community usually loses out. How many of us would pass up a lucrative promotion that involved relocation in favor of deepening our local roots? How many of us would trade the anonymity of the city (no matter how lonely at times) for the cloying, gossipy, parochial place we imagine small-town America to be? We must begin by recognizing that our verbal homage to community is only one side of a deep ambivalence that runs through the American character, on the other side of which is a celebration of unfettered individualism.

The Resurgence of Individualism

In times past, this American ambivalence was anchored strongly on two sides, for both individualism and community seemed possible. The settlers of the American frontier had to possess both the strength of individuality and the capacity for community. To survive, they needed to be able to stand alone and stand together. But in our time, individualism has run amok. We remain ambivalent, but the anchor holding us to community has been tugged loose. We find ourselves drifting dangerously toward the rocks of autonomy and the isolated self, in part because we can no longer be certain that community is available to us.

The breakdown of confidence in community has been explored by Philip Rieff in *The Triumph of the Therapeutic*.[1] Rieff argues that community itself once prevented disintegration of the individual personality, for in community, each person had a place. Absent were anxieties about whether a person was needed and where: the answers were woven into the very fabric of society. And in the event that one life, one personality, did crumble, community itself was the therapy: in community, one could find a comforting role that helped bring the self back together.

But with the breakdown of our common life came growing personal disintegration and the need for a form of therapy that did not depend on community. So a new therapeutic mode emerged—notably Freudian—whose aim was to create a self that could function without communal support, an individual who could get along without others. As Rieff notes, the development of this self is promoted both explicitly and implicitly by the therapeutic process. For example, the "crisis of transference" is the point at which the patient must learn to become independent even of the therapist. And the sheer expense of therapy is a constant reminder to the patient that support does not come freely from the community but must be purchased in the marketplace.

The assumption that community is no longer available and that we must learn to go it alone pervades other areas of modern life—for example, education. Historically, education, community, and culture were inseparable. What students learned reflected a communal consensus on what they needed to know, helping the community and its culture renew and reknit itself.

Today education has become a training ground for competition. In fact, education itself has become a competitive arena where winners and losers are determined even before the contest of adult life begins. It is not only that educational practices like grading on the curve are so obviously rooted in social Darwinism. It is not only that when students get together to collaborate on their homework, many schools call it "cheating," so suspect are the communal virtues. It is not only that adults often insist that children who are educated to cooperate rather than compete are not well prepared for the "real world." Beneath these symptoms lies the fact that the function of modern schools is more economic than cultural. They provide one more reminder that we should count not on communal support but on our individual survival skills.

The "triumph of the therapeutic"—of the premise that community is gone and we must learn to stand alone—can also be found in much that passes for spirituality these days. In religious as well as secular life, community has disappointed and failed us. As a result, many who are open to religious experience or on a spiritual quest cannot tolerate the church in any of its organized forms.

So certain forms of spirituality that emphasize the solitary journey of the self-seeking self have gathered many adherents. At their worst, these "new religions" have made the ego-self the object of the spiritual quest. Not the self that is made in God's image or the self in which can be found "that of God," as Quakers put it. No, in some of the new religions, God and the self-seeking self are taken to be one and the same: lost is the confrontation between true self and ego-self as they become absorbed into one another. Lost, too, is the sense that the self is defined by participation in communities of covenant—lost along with the confidence that anything beyond the self can be trusted.

The Risk of Seeking Community

The assumption that community is increasingly hard to find is well founded. It *is* difficult to find or create relationships of duration and reliability in our kind of world. But such realism quickly becomes pernicious: every time we act on that assumption, every time we gird ourselves to go it alone, we create more of the same.

The assumption that community cannot be counted on is a self-fulfilling prophecy, and as we act on it, we become men and women who do not call others to accountability and cannot be counted on ourselves. "Crackpot realism" is what C. Wright Mills would have called it, for its only outcome can be an accelerating decline of community.[2] We need to find the courage to assert and act on the hope that community remains a human possibility, because only by acting "as if" can we create a future fit for human habitation.

We will find that courage only as we come to a new understanding of what it means to seek health for our personal lives. We live in a time of extreme self-consciousness, a time of self-doubt, self-examination, self-help. We seem aware of every inner perturbation, as if we had been born with psychic seismographs capable of measuring each movement along our personal fault lines. Ours is a time in which personal health is supposed to come by focusing on ourselves and by seeking the resources for self-renewal.

But personal well-being is one of those strange things that eludes those who aim directly at it and comes to those who aim elsewhere. It was best said in the words of Jesus: "He who seeks his life will lose it, and he who loses his life . . . will find it" (Matthew 10:39). We must learn that the ultimate therapy for the unwell self is to identify our own pain with the pain of others and band together to resist the conditions that create our common malady.

That is, the ultimate therapy is to translate our private problems into public issues. As we try to do so, we will discover that some of our private problems are too trivial to be dignified with public status, and they will fade away. But others will turn out to be common to our time, not just private pains but collective pathologies. As we see and respond to our own plight in the lives of our sisters and brothers, we will begin to find health. Real therapy involves building relationships of shared concern. Only so can we heal ourselves.

All this inverts conventional wisdom. We fear community because we think we will lose ourselves in it, finding our selfhood overpowered by the identity of the group. We pit individuality and community against one another, and of course, we choose the former. But what a curious conception of self our fear of community reflects! How did we manage to forget that the self is a moving intersection of many other selves, formed by all the lives that interact with and enrich our own? The larger and richer one's community, the larger and richer the content of the self. Paradoxically, community and individuality go hand in hand: an affluent suburb with many lifestyle options but little community breeds less individuality than a provincial village with few choices but a rich community life.

We have lost personal well-being because we have lost community. But lost things can be found. Community can be rebuilt as more and more of us find within ourselves the need and the willingness to risk community. And as we do so, we will discover that the risk was an illusion. On the other side of our fear of community we find no risk at all, only a DNA-deep memory that life was meant to be lived together along with utter bafflement about how we ever forgot that elemental fact.

The Politics of Community

The finest form of personal therapy is to build community, and building community is the finest form of politics. So community is a place where therapy and politics meet, a place where the health of the individual and the health of the group are recognized as the reciprocal realities they are.

The link between therapy and politics becomes clear as we reflect on loneliness, that defining fact of so many modern lives that community is supposed to cure. But loneliness is not just an interpersonal problem; it has political causes and consequences. We are lonely because a mass society keeps us from engaging one another on matters of common destiny. And loneliness makes us prey to a thousand varieties of political manipulation, rendering us not only pathetic but politically dangerous as well. If we understood that fact, we might create communities that contribute to political and personal health by more fairly distributing the power of decision making over our personal and corporate destinies.

Political scientists have long known that community in its many forms plays a key role in the distribution of power. Families, neighborhoods, work groups, churches, and other voluntary associations stand between the lone individual and the power of the central state. They provide each of us with a human buffer zone so that we do not stand utterly vulnerable against the state's demands. They amplify each person's small voice so it can be heard by a state that turns deaf when it does not want to listen. And in such communities, we gain skill at negotiating our interest with the interests of the group.

If these communities decline in quantity or quality, the emergent result is a "mass society." Such a society is characterized not simply by size but by the fact that individuals in it do not have organic relationships with one another, only a common membership in the nation-state. In mass society, the person stands alone against the state, without a network of communal associations to protect personal meaning, to enlarge personal power, or to teach and learn the habits of democracy.

The loneliness of people in a mass society is a measure of their political impotence, and given that impotence, that inability to act together, the step from mass society to totalitarianism is a short one. In a totalitarian society, the state exercises careful control over the number and nature of intermediary communities to make sure that they do not encourage and empower individuals to resist the state. As true community begins to wither in a democracy, so also does the quality of democracy itself.

We sadly misconstrue politics if we focus our concern exclusively on the institutions of government and how they operate. The functioning of democratic institutions depends on the existence of a communal life—a life to which government is accountable, a life that gives people the power to make claims on those who govern. Even more fundamental, communal life is the context in which people come to understand their interrelatedness. Without that understanding, people will have no interest in government except as it impinges directly on their self-interest, and democracy will fall into disrepair. Community is a precondition of a democratic politics, and the building and maintaining of community is an essential prepolitical task.

But the American condition is one of deepening privatism. Affluence (or the desire to maintain the illusion of it) draws us into ways of living designed to protect us from the sight and sound of one another. Goods and services that we might share with or provide for one another become individual consumer items, thus weakening the communal fabric. We are more concerned about being consumers than citizens, preferring to purchase autonomy rather than revealing our interdependence.

In truth, of course, we are interdependent, despite our extensive and expensive efforts to build a facade of autonomy. But as the world economic crisis deepens, we will continue to learn just how interdependent we are, and that knowledge may reawaken us to our need for community. At the height of the "fuel shortage" of the mid-1970s, people quickly learned to share automobile transportation with their neighbors.

But that crisis passed, and the sharing passed with it. As such crises multiply, there will probably be an interim period in which old habits of competition and acquisitiveness will assert themselves with renewed vigor as people struggle to ward off the dawning knowledge that things will never be the same. It will be some time before the worldwide pressure to share becomes so great as to make community the only sensible option.

So those who cultivate the instincts of community and labor to build its external forms are engaged in a task whose success is critical to our collective future. The politics and economics of community are fundamental, and until we understand their full implications, our image of community will continue to be romantic and irrelevant. Community means more than the comfort of souls. It means, and has always meant, the survival of species.

True Community or False?

The longer we sing the praises of community, the more we court another romantic fallacy: that to say "community" is to say "good." Not so. Selma, Cicero, South Boston, and every other example of racist collectivism—these were all communities, but false ones. As we learn the difference between true community and false, we will move even further from sentimentality about the common life.

The most notable example of false community is the totalitarian society that emerges as true community declines. In the midst of mass loneliness, people yearn to identify with something larger than themselves, something that can redeem their lives from insignificance. This yearning runs so deep that even the appearance of community will feed it, so totalitarianism always presents itself as a communal feast for the masses, garnished with mythic meaning. What was Nazi Germany except a demonic form of community life? What is any brand of nationalism or racism except the archetype of community run amok?

The sociopolitical differences between true community and false could be listed at length. For instance, false communities tend to be manipulated by the state, while true communities are independent of governmental power. In true communities, people are free to relate in ways that challenge established power, while in false communities, power protects itself by setting limits on acceptable forms of association.

In false communities, the group is regarded as superior to the individual, while in true communities, both individual and group are believed to have a claim on truth. In true communities, the individual will be checked and balanced by the group and the group will be checked and balanced by the individual, for truth is not necessarily found either in majorities or in one voice crying in the wilderness. In false communities, the individual is swallowed up in ideological abstractions such as Nazi Germany's "blood, soil, and race." But true communities are built on assessments of concrete individuals, not abstractions about classes of people.

False communities tend to be homogenous, exclusive, and divisive, while true communities strive to unite persons across lines of diversity. We should be suspicious of any "community" that forms too quickly and too easily. It is likely to depend on preexisting social categories that make not for community but for commonality—and commonality does not nurture the human growth and expansiveness that true community provides.

But beyond all these sociological differences between true community and false, there is a theological way to express the differences that brings us to the heart of the matter. False communities are idolatrous. They take a finite attribute like race, creed, political ideology, or lifestyle and elevate it to ultimacy. They seek security by making absolute that which is relative, making eternal that which is temporal, by worshiping that which should be held critically. They confuse their own power with the power of God and use that power to decide questions of life and death. False communities are ultimately demonic, which is not to say that true communities are divine, for both retain their human character. But true communities will take covenantal form, experiencing both God's mercy and God's judgment over the course of time.

These categories are not fixed, for a false community can turn true and a true community can turn false. A true community is always tempted toward pride and arrogance, the preconditions of idolatry. So a true community is also a self-critical community that is always ready to deflate its pretensions before they balloon up to deity size. A true community will have mechanisms for scrutinizing its conception of whatever it holds most dear, for that is the point at which the greatest danger of idolatry occurs.

All of this reminds us again that community is ultimately a religious phenomenon. Nothing can bind together broken but willful human selves except a transcendent power. But not all powers perceived as transcendent are creative or even benign. What that power is and what it demands of those who rely on it—these are factors that determine the quality of a community's life.

Some Myths About Community

Understanding true community requires the deconstruction of several romantic myths, myths that have replaced the reality of community in contemporary thought.

First, there is the myth that community is a creature comfort that can be added to a life full of other luxuries. For the affluent, community has become yet another consumer item. You can buy it in weekend chunks at retreat centers, or you and your kind can have it by purchasing homes in a gated village.

But community is another one of those things (like personal well-being) that eludes us if we aim directly at it. Instead, community comes as a by-product of commitment and struggle.

It comes when we step forward to right some wrong, to heal some hurt, to give some service. Then we discover each other as allies in resisting the diminishments of life. It is no accident that the most impressive sense of community is found among people in the midst of such joyful travail, among those who have said no to tyranny with the yes of their lives.

Of all the myths of community, that of community as a commodity will be the hardest to overcome. The world teaches us to go after what we want directly, aggressively, single-mindedly. But community, approached that way, remains just beyond our reach. We cannot have it just because we want it, precisely because the foundation of community itself goes beyond selfishness into life for others. Only as our beliefs and acts link us to the invisible community of humankind will visible forms of community grow up around us.

Another myth equates community with utopia, misleading us into imagining that with easy access to one another, we will find ourselves brothers and sisters again. But community is less like utopia than like a crucible or a refiner's fire, not least because easy access always means the collision of egos. In this process, God wants us to learn something about ourselves, our limits, our need for others. In this process, there is the pain of not getting our way but the promise of finding a Way, as Dietrich Bonhoeffer knew well:

> Innumerable times a whole Christian community has broken down because it had sprung from a dream wish. . . .

God's grace speedily shatters such dreams. Just as surely as God desires to lead us to a knowledge of genuine Christian fellowship, so surely must we be overwhelmed by a great disillusionment with others, with Christians in general, and, if we are fortunate, with ourselves. . . . God is not a God of the emotions but the God of truth. . . . He who loves his dream of a community more than the Christian community itself becomes a destroyer of the latter, even though his personal intentions may be ever so honest and earnest and sacrificial.[3]

People who come into community, Christian or otherwise, with only their "dream wish" will soon leave—hurt, resentful, and probably lost to the cause of community building. But those who can survive the dissolution of their dream and the abrasion of their egos will find that the truth of community is richer and more supportive than fantasy can ever be. For in community, one learns that the solitary self is not an adequate measure of reality, that we can begin to know the fullness of truth only through multiple visions.

The great danger in our utopian dreams of community is that they lead us to favor association with people just like ourselves. Here we confront the third myth of community, that it will be an extension and expansion of our own egos, a confirmation of our own partial view of reality. I have often heard it argued that in a real community, a group would have absolute power to select new members and thus control the degree of dissonance within.

Not so. In a true community, we will not choose our companions, for our choices are always limited by self-serving motives. Instead, our companions will be given to us by grace, and often they will be persons who will upset our view of self and world. In fact, we might define true community as that place where the person you least want to live with always lives!

If we are willing to live with that person, we can avoid the trap that Richard Sennett has called the "purified community."[4] Here, as in the typical suburb, one is surrounded by likeness to the extent that challenge is unlikely and growth is impossible. In true community, there will be enough diversity and conflict to shake loose our need to make the world in our own image. True community will teach us the meaning of the prayer "Thy will, not mine, be done."

In exploring and exploding each of these myths we are reminded again that true community is a spiritual reality that cannot be reduced to social and psychological principles. If Martin Buber was right that in turning to each other we turn to God, then community is a context for conversion—literally, "a turning."[5]

Community can remind us that we are called to love, for community is a product of love in action and not of simple self-interest. Community can break our egos open to the experience of a God who cannot be contained by our conceptions. Community can teach us that our grip on truth is fragile and incomplete, that we need many ears to hear the fullness of God's word for our lives. And the disappointments of community life can be transformed by our discovery that the only dependable power for life lies beyond all human structures and relationships.

In this spiritual grounding lies the only real hedge against the disillusionment that community inevitably brings. That disillusionment can be borne only if it is not community one seeks but truth, light, God. Do not commit to community, but commit to that which stands beyond all human constructions. In that commitment, we will find ourselves drawn into community, and the difficult lessons community teaches can be borne and transformed into a larger and truer life.

Forms of Life Together

Community is a process of spiritual unfolding. But it is also a place. When Buber says, "We expect a theophany of which we know nothing but the place, and the place is called community," he suggests how place and process are intertwined. A theophany, an encounter with the living God, is obviously mysterious and full of movement. But for Christians and Jews, that encounter always occurs in the concrete places of this world. When we lose our sense of place, community becomes another one of those disembodied spiritual terms that excite our imaginations but fail to connect with reality.

American history has been punctuated by resurgences of the communal spirit, always accompanied by the notion that small, intentional communities, withdrawn from the larger society, are the only truly worthy form of life together. Clearly, communal experiments are important, providing models and serving as "learning labs" for less intensive forms of life together. But they are out of reach for many people. We need to help one another build community where we are, rather than encouraging dreams that turn to despair about a form of community that simply does not fit the needs of many contemporary lives. We need to foster the diverse forms of community that are needed if an urban, technological society is to recover its human roots.

Some of us are called to focus on the community called the family, whose role in the larger quest for community is clear. For many people, the family is the place where the difficulty, even the impossibility, of community is first sensed. If one grows up in a family where trust does not exist and support cannot be found, one becomes an adult fearful of further rejection, an adult who will not risk community again.

If it seems idealistic to suppose that many people will place community of any sort, including the family, ahead of personal mobility and economic advancement, consider that the prospect of shrinking world resources may force us to do exactly that. Many of us, and our children, may no longer be able to ride the "up" economic escalator, and as we stop being mobile we may learn to pay more grateful attention to what is around us. A leveling economy will compel us to share more fully than we do now, and sharing could well mean some form of extended family.

The impact of economic trends on family life is nowhere more evident than in the growing demands of women for a full and rightful share of both work and compensation. The mothering force that held the family together in earlier eras was based partly on the exclusion of women from the ranks of paid workers. As women lay claim to their economic rights, it becomes clear that men must more fully share the tasks of family maintenance if the family is to be a model of community life.

That the family can be a model of great power seems clear. For example, many of us find it impossible to imagine a form of community in which each contributes according to ability and receives according to need, a community with a common pot built up by those who can and drawn down by those who must. Yet wage earners in strong families have no question that a child or a spouse who earns no money has full claim on his or her resources. We might reach toward larger expressions of community by asking how to expand our sense of who belongs to "our family."

Beyond the family, some of us may be called to build community in our neighborhoods, which are rarely places where we practice the great commandment to "love thy neighbor." And once again, most of us want it that way. We want to protect some private space in our busy lives, to be free of entanglements with those who live next door, to live without obligation and move on without a sense of loss when necessity or opportunity calls us elsewhere.

The health of our neighborhoods is fundamental to the health of the larger body politic: without local forms of community, it is impossible for representative democracy to exist. In political terms, neighborhoods are not a nicety. They are a locus and source of citizenship, a wellspring of feelings of relatedness, responsibility, and efficacy. The political impotence so many people feel today is directly related to the failure of local community: how can one hope to influence the course of a nation if one has no microcosm in which to exercise political muscle?

In our mobile metropolitan life, it takes some external force to make a neighborhood become aware of itself as a community. In our time, one such force has been the simple fact of changing demographics, especially in the racial and economic composition of an area. For the most part, of course, such change has been viewed fearfully and defensively. It has caused false community to form, a community that tries to exclude those who are somehow different.

But more positive outcomes are possible. For five years in suburban Washington, D.C., I was involved with a project aimed at helping white middle-class people cope with community change.[6] The core of that project was a series of "living room seminars" that brought together ten or fifteen neighbors in an eight-week curriculum designed to help them identify and overcome the sources of their resistance to change.

Beneath their fears of "the other," the people in these seminars did not want to run from change. They wanted to embrace it and learn from it. But their sense of isolation made them fearful and brittle. So they set out to build community in small but practical ways. One group, for example, developed the Neighborhood Resource Catalogue, listing the interests and skills that residents would be willing to share with one another. These exchanges were community builders, of course, and so also was the simple act of going door to door asking neighbors what they might like to list in the catalogue.

Apparently we need excuses to meet our neighbors. But when we do, face to face, community begins to emerge, and our fear of "those people" begins to recede. In small but significant ways, projects such as these help neighbors become neighbors, and people are able to replace their fearful stereotypes with the human face of community.

Beyond family and neighborhoods, some of us may be called to build community in the places where we go to school and work. These have become the primary arenas of hierarchy and competition for many Americans, where we are pitted against one another so that something called "higher performance" may be achieved. But when we destroy community in the workplace, we get shoddy products and unethical practices. When we destroy the community of scholars, we get diminished forms of teaching and learning. We will build community at school and at work only when we understand that community, creativity, and achievement go hand in hand.

Most of us do not believe that collaboration is the best source of good work, for we inhabit institutions that keep reinforcing the assumption that good work comes from competition in which the instinct to win is exploited. Most of us believe that education that does not rank individuals in relation to each other is simply not rigorous enough, and we are skeptical of the assumptions about human nature that lie behind group projects where everyone wins and no one loses.

But there is considerable evidence that a well-structured group can be smarter than any of its members. I think, for example, of simulation games that pose a problem for individuals to solve on their own and then invite individuals to share and correct each other's solutions in a quest for consensus.[7] The consensus is almost always closer to the correct solution of the problem than is the solution of any individual in the group, often dramatically so.

If data such as these were taken seriously, the competitive individualism of both school and work might begin to be transformed. And with it would come not only a higher level of personal satisfaction but also a higher level of learning, creativity, and practical problem solving.

Community and the Churches

It seems ironic to suggest that some of us may be called to build community in our churches, for the church as it was meant to be is a historical archetype of community. But the church is human as well as divine, and it has clearly failed to be the kind of community God, and some of us, had in mind. And yet religious communities continue to carry great potential for true community life: the tradition and symbolism of community are there, and sometimes the leadership is there as well.

Most important, the church universal embraces a huge cross section of the world's diversity, held together—in theory—by the commitment to a truth that transcends our differences. In practice, the church too often tries to suppress the diversity it contains. But if it could learn to deal with its secondary differences in the context of its fundamental unity, the church would be our most compelling model of community.

The core of the Christian tradition is a way of inward seeking that leads to outward acts of integrity and service, acts of love. Christians are most in the Spirit when they stand at the crossing point of the inward and the outward life. And at that intersection, community is found. Community is a place where the connections felt in our hearts make themselves known in the bonds between people and where the tuggings and pullings of those bonds keep opening up our hearts.

The church can make its greatest contribution to community by persisting in its worship—by persisting, I mean, in the practice of the presence of God. Again, community is simply too difficult to be sustained by our social impulses. It can be sustained only as we return time and again to the spiritual experience of the unity of all life. To put it in Quaker terms, community happens as that of God in you responds to that of

God in me. And the affirmation that there is that of God in every person means far more than "I'm OK, you're OK." It means affirming the essential sacredness of every human life.

Our churches would do well to give more time to the sacrament of silence in our common worship. I am a garden-variety Christian, and I need to hear the words of faith spoken and affirmed. But I also know that much of religious truth is simply inexpressible and that words can divide us while truth can bring us together in silence. Among the many kinds of worshiping communities the world needs, it surely needs those that embrace diversity within a mystical truth that transcends creeds.

But in the silence of mysticism lurk dangers as well. The mystical experience of unity we may find in meditation is rarely manifest in the human world, so seekers of spiritual unity may be tempted to flee the imperfections of embodied life. Or we may be tempted to worship the silence itself, forgetting that contemplation is only a vehicle in which God may come to disrupt as well as comfort us. Both of these are temptations to idolatry, and both of them undermine community. If we forsake the vexations of human relations for the perfection of the silent life, then community—to say nothing of real life—will be impossible for us.

What we need is not simply the individual at prayer, seeking to stand in his or her own sacred space. We need a corporate practice that seeks a space in which we can all stand together. In worship, we need to know that God wants to bring us together as God's people and that we must listen to each other, in the words and in the silences between them, testing our own truth against the truth received by others. We need to know that God will work a greater truth in all of us standing together than can be worked in any one of us standing alone.

Here is where Christians can contribute to community by refusing to follow the religious individualism of our times. Behind many of the new spiritual movements lies the assumption that truth is altogether subjective: one truth for you, another for me, and never mind the difference. But when we understand truth that way, the truth we are given will have no chance to transform society or ourselves. If we affirm community, we must take the risks that our own version of truth will be enlarged or even made uncouth by the light given to other people.

If true community is to flourish, the individual must flourish as well. So as the church seeks corporate truth, it must be ever mindful of the insight that an individual can be given. In our corporate seeking, the individual must never be overpowered, never coerced into going along, never lost to membership in an outvoted and embittered minority. Christians can contribute to community by walking the way that lies between religious authoritarianism and spiritual subjectivism. As the church tests for corporate truth, it must always respect the word of God in the solitary heart, a word that may be too radical for the group to hear.

The truth Christians have been given has led them into some of the hard places of history, places where truth must speak to power, and in these places, a living experience of community has been found. Mildred Binns Young has written of the communal life among the first generation of Quakers who brought suffering after suffering upon themselves simply by living out the light of Christ that dwelt within them. She speaks of the fact that under these "all but annihilating persecutions" Quakers "drew people to them as [they] never have since."[8]

Those Friends did not have to devise fancy schemes for generating a community life. Instead, "their necessities kept them together"—such necessities as the need to care for members who had been imprisoned and for their stranded children; the need to share what few animals and tools were left after the tax collectors had confiscated most of them; the need to petition authorities for relief from injustice. "So," writes Mildred Binns Young, "a Friends meeting, without any theories of communalism, had in effect something like it."[9]

Theory can only provide clues. Community comes from faithful living. If Christians can lead such lives in the context of family and neighborhood, of school and workplace, and in the body politic, we can contribute to the creation of a community both human and divine. There is no witness more urgent for our day.

CHAPTER V

A World of Scarcity, a Gospel of Abundance

Scarcity and abundance are fundamental concepts in the political and economic travail of our times. The world is split into "haves" and "have-nots," into those who have more than enough to eat and stay warm and those who lack even the minimum to survive. With predictions of dwindling natural resources and growing pessimism over technology's ability to bridge the gap, even we "haves" have begun to know fear. And in our fear, we consume and hoard even more, further unbalancing the scales of global justice.

These things are widely known. But it may not be commonly understood that scarcity and abundance are also fundamental concepts in our spiritual lives. We have not talked enough about the connection between our state of spiritual awareness and our ability to respond to political and economic wrongs. The quality of our contemplation dictates, to a considerable extent, whether we find life pinched and cramped and fearful or open, expansive, and free. If our inner life is one of scarcity and grasping, we will surely not live an outward witness to a just and merciful sharing of the earth's goods.

In this essay, I want to examine the world's logic of scarcity and God's promise of abundance. I want to look at scarcity and abundance as aspects of the spiritual quest. And I want to suggest three ways in which we can help ourselves and each other move from the life-destroying habits of scarcity toward the life-affirming instincts of abundance: the ways of education, community, and prayer.

The Scarcity Assumption

More than we know, our lives are governed by rules—not the rules of civil society but rules that flow from the assumptions we make about life. Each of us is filled with such assumptions, with beliefs about "how things are" and what we can expect. Our attitudes and behaviors are shaped by these beliefs, beliefs we rarely examine because, if we are aware of them at all, we think they simply reflect reality.

If we believe life is a jungle, then that's the way life is likely to be for us, not because life really is a jungle but because the assumption leads us to act in ways that cause the jungle to grow up around us. The paranoid person eventually creates the very enemies that began only in his or her imagination. These prophecies come true not because they are inevitable but because we bring them to life by acting *as if* they were true.

So it is with scarcity and abundance. Are the basic goods of life plentiful or in short supply? It depends on your assumptions. What do you assume those basic goods to be? If diamonds are vital to you, scarcity becomes a problem. And what do you assume about the sources of supply? If all of life's goods must be obtained through cash exchange with others, it will be hard to see the abundance that lies beyond dependence on the market.

Most people seem to assume that scarcity is a simple fact of life. How else can one explain the obsession with acquiring, consuming, and hoarding that permeates our society? We live in constant fear of the future, the fear that money will run out, that food supplies will dwindle, that housing will be unavailable. And when we act on those fears, the assumption becomes reality: as we consume more than we need and hoard against our fears about the future, stores do dwindle, prices do rise, and there will be too little to go around.

The tragic victims of this self-fulfilling prophecy are, of course, the have-nots of the world who lack the capital to act out their economic fears. For them, scarcity is no assumption at all: it is a hard and cruel fact of life. But that fact is created by people who have a choice—the choice to assume scarcity and grab for all one can get or the choice to assume abundance and live in such a way as to create and share it. For those of us who are affluent and educated, choosing assumptions is no mere academic exercise or mental workout. The lives of others, and our own souls, hang in the balance.

The Reality of Abundance

As we look at nature, at what is freely given to us in creation, we cannot help but be impressed with its abundance. Properly treated, nature seems capable of infinite self-renewal and replenishment. Seeds grow in fertile soil; animals multiply apace; the soil is re-created by the death of flora and fauna; the earth is fecund beyond imagination. And what nature does not supply ready-made, a humane technology is able to fabricate: amalgams and compounds and derivatives for meeting our every need. Set aside for a moment our misuse of the earth and the madness that surrounds our technology and simply contemplate the abundance of nature and human inventiveness, in their right order.

In the midst of such abundance, how can we explain the scarcity assumption? When we are surrounded by a grace that is capable of meeting reasonable human needs, how did we end up with things in short supply?

One answer lies in our tendency to overvalue things according to the whims of ego and culture. When we exaggerate the importance of something, hinging our happiness on our ability to own it, and when thousands of us are obsessed with the same thing at the same time, that thing becomes scarce, either because supplies become depleted or the price soars beyond most people's reach.

Another answer lies in our habit of arbitrarily limiting the sources of supply. Food can be grown almost anywhere black earth can be found. But when we insist on devoting much of that earth to lawns or covering it over with shopping malls and parking lots, we limit agriculture and make its issue scarce. It is not that nature has become less generous but that we have chosen to reject her gifts.

What is truly remarkable about the human animal is not that we take physical abundance and turn it into scarcity but that we do the same with the infinite gifts of the Spirit! It is one thing to overvalue diamonds or undersupply tomatoes. It is quite another thing to treat love, affection, trust, and regard as if they were scarce. And yet how many of us do exactly that? How often in our relationships do we act as if the stores of love were limited and if others get too much of it, there will be too little left for me? Here is the basis of all human jealousies and envies, this instinct that there are not enough of these "Spirit goods" to go around.

Or take a human good like pleasure. Clearly, ways of having fun are infinite in number, limited only by our imaginations. But how many of us spend weekends and summers resenting that we lack the money to *really* have fun or that all the money we spent failed to buy enough of the "happiness product"? We have limited the supply of fun by putting the power to produce it in the hands of sports promoters, casino operators, and travel agents. We have put ourselves in the position of anxious and impoverished consumers wanting to buy from the approved sources but with never enough cash or satisfaction to come out ahead. We have made what is obviously abundant into something that is scarce.

Or take another intangible: education. Clearly, education is a boundless adventure of the human spirit, possible in any place, under any circumstance, with any material one can imagine. What are the limits on learning or teaching? There are none. Why, then, have we put boundaries around education, called the result "schools," and made schooling an object of bitter competition? Why have we taken what is limitless in human experience and made it scarce, creating a situation in which people's self-esteem, and too often the course of their lives, is determined by the fact that some get more and some get less?

The Dynamics of Scarcity

Why indeed? The more one presses that question, the more puzzling it becomes. Once we recognize that many of the scarcities we suffer from are self-imposed, and once we recognize how this brings us only to grief, the more we have to wonder why we willfully choose the lesser portion.

For those of us who are affluent and educated, it is too easy to blame the scarcity game on the politics and economics of greed. Clearly, greed is at work. If you can convince people that they need something and limit and control its supply, you have either power or wealth, and the one leads to the other. So there is self-interest, for some, in creating scarcities where none exist, and self-interest is ample explanation for any human behavior.

But the self-interest of some does not explain why the rest of us succumb to their definitions of scarcity. Just because someone wants to gain power and wealth by trying to promote an illusion of scarcity, why should we accept the illusion? Why do we let the monarchs of scarcity walk down the streets naked without ever shouting, "The king has no clothes!"?

The answer to that question probes to the deepest level of our spiritual condition. For our devotion to the illusion of scarcity—and again, I refer to those of us who have a choice— is more than mere politics or economics. At bottom, it has to do with our sense of identity. Most of us gain our sense of self not from what we share with others but from the ways we are different from them. I define myself not in terms of what you and I have in common but by what I have that you don't and what you have that I don't. I define myself in relation to the scarcities that differentiate us.

Somewhere, deep within us, we fear commonality. We want to be unique, different, individual. We hardly notice aspects of ourselves in which we are similar, but we are sharply aware of the ways in which we are different—in appearance, education, status, wealth. When we meet, we quickly ask for evidence of our differences: What do you do? Where did you go to school? Behind it all is the weighing and the measuring, the assessment of who has more and who has less, the search for our distinctions.

Why the need to feel different, to distinguish ourselves from the mass? Perhaps because sameness seems like a kind of death to us, a sort of drowning in the sea of humanity. We are always struggling to keep our heads above water, to "stand out" from the community as if this would save our lives. In fact, as every swimmer knows, the trick is to relax into the water and rely on its ability to support a body that does not fight it. But we so fear the death of our distinctions that we fight to rise above the very medium of common humanity that would hold us up.

In theological terms, I am speaking here of the problem of idolatry. For by gaining identity from the possession of scarce goods, we are establishing those goods as gods in our lives. We give these gods the power to make us happy or miserable; the power to discriminate among people, separating the worthy from the unworthy, the better from the worse. By attaching our identity to things only a few can have, we ignore the intrinsic preciousness of all human life. Worse still, we help maintain a social structure that gives some people an exaggerated sense of worth while discouraging others from ever feeling worthy at all.

The Gospel of Abundance

For those of us who are relatively affluent, scarcity and abundance turn out to be spiritually rooted issues, not conditions external to our lives. When we cling to the world's resources—material or otherwise—we create external scarcity. But that scarcity is a reflection of our inner condition, a condition in which we try to make meaning and assuage our fears by clinging. Of course, the more we cling, the more meaning recedes and fear triumphs: no matter how much we have, we always "need" more.

In contrast to this grasping at life is the emphasis on "letting go" that is central to all great spiritual traditions. In Zen Buddhism, the path is one of constantly emptying the vessel, of not letting the mind hold on to any idea or experience or desire or image. In all the Eastern meditative disciplines, the key is to relax and release the will, to let go of all false securities, in order to rest in the power of reality and truth.

The same path is found at the heart of Christianity. At the core of the Gospel, there is a constant emphasis on trusting God's abundance and living beyond our fears of scarcity. "See how the lilies grow," says Jesus,

> they do not toil, or spin, and yet I tell you that even Solomon in all his glory was not arrayed like one of these. If God, then, so clothes the grasses which live today in the fields and will feed the ovens tomorrow, will he not

be much more ready to clothe you, men of little faith? You should not be asking, then, what you are to eat or drink, and living in suspense of mind; it is for the heathen world to busy itself over such things; your Father knows well that you need them. No, make it your first care to find the kingdom of God, and all these things shall be yours without the asking. (Luke 12:26–31)

At the heart of letting go is faith and trust. If we do not trust that God "knows well that you need them," we will grasp at life's necessities and even at luxuries. Lacking faith that God will provide, we can only hoard against an uncertain tomorrow. But what is the warrant for trust when the world is full of examples that would make trust the lifestyle of fools? Is it not prudent to be suspicious, to take nothing for granted, to compete for more than our share, to hoard against future threats? As long as even a minority of people operate this way, they create a climate in which trust itself seems untrustworthy.

Perhaps this situation—with its self-fulfilling anxieties and its illusions of material security—is part of God's providence. For it is precisely by thinking that we can buy our security, and then by experiencing the loss of all that "moth and rust doth corrupt," that most of us are given a chance at conversion. Most of us learn about the paradox of scarcity and abundance only when we are broken in our efforts to put money or status or material well-being in that cavern of need that can only be filled by God.

And what is this paradox? Simply that "he who seeks his life shall lose it, and he who loses his life . . . shall find it." True abundance comes not to those set on securing wealth but to those who are willing to share apparent scarcity in a way that creates more than enough. Those who seek well-being, who grasp for more than their share, will find life pinched and fearful. They will reap only the anxiety of needing more and more, fueled by the fear that someday everything will be taken away. But those who reach out in service to their brothers and sisters, knowing that true abundance is found not in hoarding but in community, will find a life of plenty. Having been there for others, they have reason to believe that others will be there for them.

Surely this is a conversion—literally, "a turning"—for it takes the world's logic of scarcity and turns it upside down. Grasping brings less; letting go brings more. What God wants from our fear of scarcity is not a voracious capitalism but the spiritual insight that we cannot buy the identity and security we seek. Those will come to us only as we let go and live in God's grace, which means living in solidarity with those for whom scarcity is no illusion but a matter of life and death.

As we who have more than enough move toward this solidarity, we will learn that people who live with material scarcity often understand spiritual abundance far better than we do. These people, who have always had to transcend in trust the world of scarce resources, will turn out to be our guides on the spiritual journey. They are the ones to whom Jesus was closest. They are the last whom the Gospel makes first. In their lives, the paradox of scarcity and abundance is made manifest for all who have ears to hear and eyes to see.

The Way of Education

How can we move beyond the self-fulfilling prophecy of scarcity into a world of shared abundance? I want to speak first about the way called education.

It is ironic that education, whose outcome should be intelligence—a quality that, rightly understood, is abundant in human nature—has become an engine of scarcity in our society. Today, the primary function of our schools is to hand out credentials that entitle some people to more and others to less of life's rewards, material and nonmaterial, including access to desirable jobs, wealth, and power. And in support of this social function, the educational process itself has become a competition over scarce resources.

In a class of fifty students, it should be possible for a teacher to award fifty A's at the end of a term. Indeed, it should be a measure of good teaching to be able to do it! And yet this rarely happens, except in places where grade inflation has set in and A's are meaningless. Instead, we have the absurdity of "grading on the curve," a system in which only a small percentage of the grades can be A's, a somewhat larger percentage B's, the largest group C's, followed by a few D's and F's. But what could be more abundant than the potential for understanding? And what could be more ludicrous and tragic than a system that forces people to compete over this plentiful commodity as if there were not enough to go around? Nowhere is there a better illustration of how we take abundance and create scarcity, driven by our belief that that competition is the best way to determine who gets what, never mind the fact that competition creates abundance for the winners and scarcity for the losers.

Of course, we want our schools to turn out people who are competent at certain jobs, such as skilled surgeons. But why do we reward only a few students for exceptional effort and punish those who fall short by comparison, fearing that if we do not make them compete, our surgeons will be hacks? Because we are quite certain that competence is in short supply and that only a few can attain it.

The outcome, of course, is medical schools in which cheating is a survival tactic for too many and a medical industry that not only exploits the consumer but falls far short of the quality one might expect in a country as affluent as ours. The prophecy of scarcity fulfills itself in our short supply of doctors (especially in less lucrative markets) and the high price of medical services, to say nothing of health care professionals who do not know how to collaborate for the sake of the patient's well-being. Where we might educate doctors in ways that create abundant public health, we instead train them in habits of competition and scarcity that diminish us all.

The true calling of the educator is to be a midwife of abundance. The classical definition of education—the Latin *educare* means to "draw out"—gives us the image we need, for the resource education works with is within each person, waiting to be brought forth.

Once again, assumptions are critical—in this case, our assumptions about human nature. I assume that each person contains all the potentials that education wishes to cultivate: insight, capacity for observation and analysis, ability to appreciate, creative energy. The trick is to create enough trust and self-affirmation to release those potentials. But conventional education seems to assume either that people don't have these potentials and must be supplied with them from without or that human nature perversely refuses to fulfill its potential and must be coerced into doing so. Research has shown that students who are assumed by their teachers to be stupid do poorly, while students assumed to be bright do well—despite the fact that the students in question represent a normal range of academic abilities. Which shall we choose: scarcity or abundance?

The transition from scarcity to abundance in education is made especially difficult by our obsession with a single form of intelligence: cognitive rationality. Our schools rank people along this one dimension, thus creating a competitive zero-sum game and the reinforcement of scarcity thinking so injurious to real learning. But some people know best with their logical minds, others with their intuition, and still others with their hands. Some people experience life in signs and symbols; others are more gifted at perceiving color and texture and form. Some learn through contemplation, while others learn largely through action and engagement. Why not recognize and cultivate the diverse ways in which people learn and know? Why not turn our schools into places where this great abundance of human intelligences is nurtured and celebrated and used?

That possibility can begin with a single teacher, a teacher willing to turn from the well-mapped highway of competition over scarce resources and walk the less charted path of educational abundance. But doing so involves trust that abundance can be found, and trust always entails risk.

The risk in this case begins with the fact that conventional education puts the teacher in command, doling out scarce information that only he or she controls. In teaching for abundance, premised on the assumption that students bring knowledge to class, the teacher loses some control by sharing power with the students; at times, the class may be teaching the teacher. Under these circumstances, some teachers have difficulty maintaining a sense of identity, having become accustomed to gaining personal identity by depriving students of theirs.

Teaching for abundance also risks meeting with resistance from students. Teachers find this problem especially painful, since they changed their way of teaching "for the students' sake." But conventional education, though it subjugates students, also puts them in a comfortable and protected position where they need never expose what they know or feel but can passively absorb what the teacher hands out. In teaching for abundance, students must come forth, be vulnerable, and respond to others. And that poses a threat that students can resent and resist.

There is risk, too, in the reactions of colleagues toward those who try to teach for abundance. Conditioned to think of education as a competitive scramble for scarce resources, the turn toward abundance can arouse suspicion and distrust. Teachers who abandon the "discipline" of pouring "content" into "empty minds" are suspected of everything from sloth to incompetence. Methods of teaching that make students into teachers and teachers into students are often ridiculed as little more than "rap sessions." It is true that these experimental pedagogies can be less than precise: we have little experience with them, and they set students and teachers alike against powerful currents of habit and tradition. But only by risking pedagogical mistakes can we start to grow modes of teaching and learning that allow the abundance of human intelligence to come forth.

All of this reminds us that education at its best is an essentially spiritual enterprise. It deals with the deepest questions of life; it demands risks that require trust; it can evoke the most inward resources of individual and group. The spiritual journey takes us toward an abundance that responds to our deepest needs. Education becomes part of that journey when it rejects the notion that intelligence and its rewards are scarce and embraces the fact that these goods are abundant and available to all.

The Way of Community

Much of what I have said about education assumes that it must become more communal, less individualistic, and less competitive if it is to become a path toward abundance. But community deserves separate consideration, for it is a potential not only at school but at home, in our neighborhoods and workplaces, and throughout the civil society. And like education, community is a spiritual matter at bottom.

From one point of view, community is simply a survival need for the years ahead, a means of sharing goods and services more widely than our privatized lives permit. Why should each family on the block have its own power mower when one industrial unit could serve a dozen families without strain? In some cities, food cooperatives have become popular for the same reason: Why should families go to the store one by one when they could reduce costs by banding together and purchasing in bulk? So community is partly a way of squeezing abundance out of dwindling resources by sharing them more fully.

But community seems impossible on practical grounds alone. Our egotism is too powerful, our individualism too deep-rooted, to maintain mere marriages of convenience. For community to endure, it must gather at a deeper level, a level that can only be called spiritual. When we are brought together by a shared sense of God's abundant love, then our sometimes scarce love for one another will not tear us apart.

That bond becomes especially strong when what calls a community into being is the desire to share God's love with the least among us—the hungry, the ill-clothed, the homeless. So community is an expression of abundance, the overflow of God's love for us. And community is an engine of abundance as well, an abundance that comes when we pool what little each of us has and find that the whole is greater than the sum of its parts. In community, we have a chance to learn that love, trust, and respect grow as you give them away; in community, we have a chance to learn that everyone is worthy of such regard.

Learning of that sort is enhanced when we are engaged with each other in a full round of daily life rather than a sharply specialized division of labor. Many needs must be met for an intentional community to function: there are meals to be prepared and dishes to be washed; there are crises to be weathered and decisions to be made; there is money to be gathered and money to be spent; there are study and worship and simply caring for one another. The strongest community is one where each person plays a part in all of these functions.

As people come together to pool what they do and do not know in each of these areas, we soon learn about the abundance and variety of human gifts. We learn that the person who is so helpful in a crisis is not a leader in daily routine.

We see that the person who cannot seem to make a decision is a powerful guide in worship. We learn that our gifts vary, with each person possessing some of what we need but no one possessing it all. We learn that the resources we need are present in the group and that the group need only establish the conditions that allow them to be freely offered.

In a strong community, the needs of life are not usually met by imports from the outside. They are evoked, and sometimes demanded, from within the community itself. A strong community will not have a resident psychoanalyst to deal with the life crises of its members. Instead, its members will be thrown back on their own resources to learn to love one another. It is remarkable how much exists within us that we never discover until conditions require it, and in a real community, those conditions keep recurring!

A community consists not of specialized professionals but of generalized amateurs. It is worth recalling that the root meaning of *amateur* is "lover," one who acts out of love for what one is doing. Love is ultimately the source of all abundance in life, and when love flows from us, our abundance becomes clear. The key to curing is caring: it seems more and more obvious that the pathologies of our era will be cured not by professionals who keep their services scarce but by amateurs who care and give in abundance.

Embedded in these reflections on community are a few clues to a major question of our time: how to turn our large, impersonal institutions in a more communal direction. Each of the marks of community I have explored here is the converse of what characterizes an institution. Where a community performs multiple functions, an institution performs one or two. Where members of a community share in all the work, an institution is based on a sharp division of labor. Where a community cultivates generalized amateurs, an institution breeds specialized professionals.

An institution can become more communal by embracing a wider range of functions and inviting its members to perform some of them for one another. Colleges, for example, constantly undercut the possibility of community by providing specialists to do all the work—preparing food, hauling garbage, caring for the grounds, cleaning the buildings, and so on. If any portion of these activities were given over to staff and students, a college would move closer to being a community. It would begin to discover the abundance of gifts that exist among its members and be reminded of an important educational fact: if we do not honor our plumbers as well as our philosophers, neither our pipes nor our theories will hold water.[1]

Obviously, it would take no less than the movement of the Holy Spirit to persuade faculty and students to share in these chores! I say that not merely in jest but as a reminder that community depends on people feeling the movement of the Spirit in their lives. And in our time, the Spirit seems to be abroad in the land. There is a hunger for community among us, to live beyond anxiety about scarcity into a shared abundance.

The Way of Prayer

If we are to transform our fear of scarcity into the good news of abundance, we must return time and again to the foundation of the spiritual life: prayer. I do not mean "saying our prayers," which sometimes seems to mean special pleading that God grant me a scarce resource before someone else gets it. I mean a life that returns constantly to that silent, solitary place within us where we encounter God and life's abundance becomes manifest.

The active life has a way of making us feel dependent on things. We need a vote here, a meal there, some money or some transportation or some support. In the frenzy of doing daily business in the world, we are seduced into believing that we are totally dependent on the world's resources, which means playing by the world's rules. These rules tell us that what we need to survive and succeed is in very short supply, and we had better hustle faster than the next person lest we lose the game.

A life of prayer is a life that constantly returns us to a place removed, where the claims of the world of scarcity fall away and are seen for the illusions they are. This is the heart of prayer, this journey from illusion to truth. And of all the illusions we must contend with, the illusion of scarcity is one of the most pernicious. As we settle into deep listening for God's word, how ludicrous the grasping ways of daily life become! In that silence and solitude, alone with the Alone, the world's version of scarcity is seen as a snare and a delusion, while God's promise of abundance comes to us not as future possibility but as a present reality.

Perhaps this is the most amazing destination of the way of prayer, this understanding that the abundance we want and need is around us and within us, here and now. We need only turn toward it and live our lives in ways that make it manifest.

CHAPTER VI

The Conversion of Knowledge

The apostle Paul was a great teacher. His teaching of a God who became human was radical, his listeners were often hostile, and yet even now, his teaching is worth attending to. History has not dismissed it, and neither can we.

Every Christian is called to be a teacher in some way. That call takes some of us into the classrooms of schools and universities. Others teach in the family or in the community or in the workplace. If it is true, as Christians believe, that "in Christ all things are made new," then we must try to understand how our faith might renew our sense of what it means to teach.

The second chapter of Paul's first letter to the church at Corinth can be read as a tract on teaching and learning, as powerful today as when it was written. In it, Paul describes his own teaching, its sources and style, in ways that recall Alfred North Whitehead's assertion that all true education is religious education.[1] Paul talks about the inner qualities a student must possess if he or she is to learn deeply and well, reminding us why we often have trouble learning. And Paul's contrast between inspired teaching and the sophistic wisdom of his day has clear parallels in our own academic culture.

Paul's words convey a vision of education whose impact is only strengthened by the fact that it is nearly two thousand years old: a vision still vibrant after so many centuries is surely grounded in something of substance. Whether we teach in the classroom or elsewhere, we can learn from Paul. He addresses timeless questions of where truth comes from and how it touches us, questions to be held close to the heart of all who are called to teach and learn.

I

> As for me, brothers, when I came to you, it was not with any
> show of oratory or philosophy, but simply to tell you what God
> had guaranteed. (1 Corinthians 2:1)

The word *professor* originally meant someone who professed a faith. To be a professor was to proclaim confidence in a power beyond all human devising, a firm ground on which to stand. Today, the role of the professor is to qualify truth claims with cautions, to acclimate students to ambiguity. The most common experience of many college students is to have the ground removed from under their feet, not to be shown a place to stand. For the most part, professors today are not people who can tell you "what God had guaranteed"!

Perhaps this is why the "show of oratory" Paul writes about is so prominent in the academy. I am reminded of the lecturer whose notes contained this marginal comment: "Point weak here—speak louder"! When relativity reigns, how else does one convince except by techniques of persuasion and even power? Professors who have nothing to profess will soon find themselves engaged in something more like posturing.

For all of this, Paul would be the last to deny the importance of having the ground pulled out from beneath one's feet. His experience on the road to Damascus—where everything he had previously believed and taught was overthrown—was easily as shattering as a freshman's first exposure to philosophy![2] But Paul's Damascus shake-up did not come not from sophistic oratory; it came from an encounter with the living Spirit by whom Paul was seized and addressed.

Surely Paul would agree that authentic education involves the destruction of myths and the disillusion of false beliefs, for had he not gone through that crucible, he would have remained Saul. But if learning is to occur, the student who is shaken must also hear hope and promise, the promise that fresh insight will come into the lives of those who are willing to be broken open. Great teachers will not just shatter our illusions. They will also bear embodied witness to the knowledge that there is a deeper place to stand when the ground beneath our feet gives way.

II

During my stay with you, the only knowledge I claimed to have was about Jesus, and only about him as the crucified Christ.
(1 Corinthians 2:2)

How our teaching would be transformed if we spoke only what we really knew! We would probably speak less, but our speaking would have new power. The listener would know that our words come from experience, that they are grounded in something that has been verified in our lives. For this is how Paul knew Christ: as a living presence in his life, a power that had grasped him and turned his life around. And this was the power of Paul's teaching, that his words reflected something that had happened to him, and his words pointed beyond himself to the source of that something.

It is well understood in the hardest of the hard sciences that words and concepts must be anchored in experience—for experiments are, after all, only a controlled form of experience. Perhaps it is primarily in the social sciences and the humanities that language sometimes springs loose from life, leaving teachers free to build worlds that are merely verbal, leaving students lost in a world that they cannot recognize as their own.

Worse still, for too many academics, teachers and students alike, studying something becomes a substitute for experiencing it. Because we have talked about poverty, we think we have engaged poverty; because we have talked about justice, we think we have done justice. When our teaching and learning get split off from experiential knowledge, we foster the great illusion that to have thought about a thing is to have lived it!

I know a teacher who has two rules in her classroom: one, speak only when you feel you must speak; and two, speak only what you truly know or ask what you truly want to know. In her classroom, there are sometimes long periods of silence, pauses that would intimidate the typical teacher and student. But here the silence is a waiting in expectation and hope that the experiential kind of truth that Paul learned and taught can be ours as well. When a silence of that sort is broken, we have more confidence that it is worthwhile to listen with care.

III

Far from relying on any power of my own, I came among you in great "fear and trembling," and in my speeches and the sermons that I gave, there were none of the arguments that belong to philosophy; only a demonstration of the power of the Spirit. And I did this so that your faith should not depend on human philosophy but on the power of God. (1 Corinthians 2:3–5)

Paul understands that as a teacher, he is, at best, the channel for a teaching that comes from beyond him, that is larger than him, that left to his own devices he could not convey. He understands that it is possible for our own willfulness to get in the way of our teaching, to so impress—or depress!—the listener with a human show of style or technique that nothing of the Spirit can come through.

But what is most remarkable here is Paul's understanding that his brokenness, his "fear and trembling," can contribute to the power of his teaching rather than inhibit it. When the teacher is transparent in this way, the student is given living testimony to the fact that God works in and through human limitation and frailty. Here is trustworthy evidence that the Spirit comes into lives that are broken open: not the teacher's words alone but the fact that this broken-open teacher can serve as the channel of a healing communication. I am reminded of another passage from Paul: "We have this treasure in earthen vessels, to show that the transcendent power belongs to God and not to us" (2 Corinthians 4:7).

Paul's comments offer no comfort to a teacher whose "brokenness" involves incompetence, inattention, or lack of preparation. When Paul says he relies on no power of his own, he is not advocating "winging it." He tells us that he came to his teaching "in great 'fear and trembling,'" which means he felt the great weight of his calling and took it with ultimate seriousness. Paradoxically, to take teaching with ultimate seriousness is to understand that it is truth who teaches, not you: it is to get the ego out of the way. This can happen only as the teacher is able to profess a living truth, a truth embodied in the teacher's true self. It can happen only as the teacher is able to pray, in his or her own way, that "God's will, not mine, be done."

IV

> But still we have a wisdom to offer those who have reached
> maturity: not a philosophy of our age, it is true, still less
> of the masters of our age, which are coming to their end.
> (1 Corinthians 2:6)

Those of us who teach in schools may be unsettled by the
notion that Paul's teaching is for "those who have reached
maturity," accustomed as we are to thinking of teaching and
learning as a process in which students mature. But how often
is teaching made difficult because our students do not yet know
enough to be teachable?

There is more to life than education, and some of this
"more" must happen before education can take hold. Paul
Goodman once said that college ought to be a place where
people go *after* they have learned something, so they can have a
chance to reflect on it! College classrooms are always more alive
when they contain people who have been out of school long
enough to know that school is not the only venue for learning.

Maturity for Paul is not about having all the answers.
Indeed, that posture toward life is a kind of death, for it closes
one off from those surprises called revelation. Instead, Paul
links maturity with the recognition that the "philosophy of our
age" and the "masters of our age" are "coming to their end."
Apparently, the wise person is one who recognizes the inad-
equacy of conventional wisdom, the hollowness of popular

conceptions of truth. The beginning of wisdom, for Paul, is not answering but questioning the established order, be it intellectual or political.

There is an important clue about teaching here, because we who teach so often fall into the trap of giving the answer without waiting for the question. The root meaning of the word *education* is "drawing out"—not simply offering new information but drawing out knowledge, conscious or otherwise, that the student already possesses: even the most callow young person has experience that can be evoked as grist for the educational mill. Giving answers rarely draws people out, but asking questions does. Under sympathetic questioning, we often realize that we know more than we thought we did or get clues as to what we need to know.

The wise person, according to Paul, is not content to be merely a skeptic, a cynic, or a naysayer, as appropriate as those attitudes may be in the face of conventional wisdom. Wisdom means a readiness for new truth, an openness to the Spirit that responds to the questions of our hearts beyond all socially sanctioned versions of what is true.

V

It is a wisdom that none of the masters of our age have ever known, or else they would not have crucified the Lord of Glory. (1 Corinthians 2:8)

We hold education in high regard in our society largely because it is a route to mastery and power, status and wealth. Through education, we hope to gain mastery at least over our own lives and ultimately over other people and events. We boast that "knowledge is power," revealing the link we have forged between teaching and learning on the one hand and controlling life on the other.

Of course, it is an illusion to believe that we control life. More than that, it is self-idolatry. The power of life, though in us, is beyond us. It is a power we can never possess but can only set ourselves for or against. In Paul's time, those who had been seduced by secular power and wished to maintain control were the ones who crucified Jesus. The light of truth will always reveal the arrogance of those who take power for their own self-serving ends—and they will always try to extinguish that light, to crucify whoever identifies with the powerless.

Sadly, education is sometimes complicit in the continuing crucifixion, especially when we use it to reinforce the social distinction between "winners" and "losers," between rich and poor. While education at its best offers opportunities for social mobility, it too often fails to serve those who are poor and hungry and naked and imprisoned. We have been told that whatever we do for the least of these, our brethren, we do for Christ. An educational system complicit in making the poor even poorer is a system that crucifies Christ again.

For Paul, right teaching aims at cultivating reverence, not power. And reverence begins in the knowledge that the only source of true power is in God, a power that builds and heals rather than injures and destroys. This reverence then takes us toward the knowledge that all people are gifted and loved by God, that all deserve an opportunity to live fully and well.

VI

> We teach what scripture calls "the things that no eye has seen and no ear has heard, things beyond the mind of man, all that God has prepared for those who love him." (1 Corinthians 2:9)

So much schooling deals only with things that the eye can see and the ear can hear. We educate for life on the surface, not life in the depths. When we leave the shallows of school and enter the depths of life, many of us have to unlearn much of what we have been taught in school and learn for the first time what is good and true and beautiful. Some do not relearn quickly enough and find themselves floundering or drowning in waters that their education never charted.

But the fact that much truth lies beyond the world of appearances, the world available to the senses, is well known, even in the hard sciences. What scientists ultimately deal with are not only observations but concepts about those observations, probes into the mystery of matter, a mystery that can be penetrated only by theory and then only approximately. Great science and reverence for mystery often walk hand in hand, and it is not all that hard to find scientists who would agree with Paul that there is much that lies "beyond the mind of man."

But Paul goes further when he suggests that the truth he teaches is available only to those who love God. What an extraordinary thing, to link knowledge and love. In our time, knowing and loving are often regarded as opposites: knowing is a function of the rational mind, and loving is an affair of the nonrational heart. But in the biblical world, the verb *know* was used to indicate intimacy. People of the Book understood that deep knowledge comes only from the inter-penetration of the knower and the known and that truth, like a person, will allow itself to be known only as the knower approaches it with love.

At the heart of Christianity is the claim that truth is personal, a claim initially found in the words of Jesus, "I am the way and the truth and the life" (John 14:6). Great teaching invites the student into a personal relation-ship with a subject, a knowing relationship—and at its best, the relationship of the knower and the known parallels the relationship of the lover and the beloved. Only so can we truly know.

Far from being "mere poetry" or antiquated understand-ing, this approach to knowing is consistent with much of con-temporary epistemology. Subatomic physics has taught us that the very presence of an observer has an impact on the observed, and philosophers of science tell us that it is impossible to separate the two. Our knowledge—far from requiring antiseptic distance between the knower and the known—would not be possible if we were not in intimate relationship with the things we seek to know.

VII

> These are the very things that God has revealed to us through the Spirit, for the Spirit reaches the depths of everything, even the depths of God. After all, the depths of a man can only be known by his own spirit, not by any other man, and in the same way the depths of God can only be known by the Spirit of God.
> (1 Corinthians 2:10–11)

For Paul, knowledge comes when spirit speaks to spirit. If we wish to know something in depth, only a dialogue of spirits will do. We must learn to look and listen beneath the surface, beyond appearance, where the spirit of a thing may be known. We must wait for that spirit to reveal itself and not try to force our way in. And we must bring our own spirit along, for only spirit can understand the things of the spirit.

But our culture has taught us to fear the personal implications of deep knowing, so we stay on the surface of things, regarding only the things we can measure as real and "spirit" as a primitive delusion. We believe that "objectivity" is the most desirable characteristic of knowledge and that we can achieve it by keeping our distance from the thing to be known so that our knowledge will be uncontaminated by personal contact. We want knowing to be a kind of spectator sport in which we do not need to get personally involved but can merely sit and observe.

Behind this insistence on objectivity is our fear that knowing in relationship means risking being known and being changed. And so it does! When knowledge comes through spirit speaking to spirit, then our spirit is searched out, and our lives may well be changed. The kind of knowledge Paul speaks of here is no spectator sport. It is a dialogue with truth in which we come to know truth and truth comes to know us—and in such knowing there is the power to challenge and change our lives.

Paul puts all this beautifully toward the end of this first letter to the church at Corinth. Speaking of the knowledge that will come when we see God face to face, he says, "The knowledge that I have now is imperfect; but then I shall know as fully as I am known" (1 Corinthians 13:12).

Philosophers assume that we can know the nature of reality because both reality and our minds have a rational structure, and reason can know reason. Paul believed that we can know what is true because truth is personal and we are persons. Just as we can love only because we are loved, so we can know only because we are known. God's Spirit reaches out to us constantly, in love and in truth, wanting to teach us, wanting us to learn. This is the assurance on which Paul's teaching rests.

VIII

> Now instead of the spirit of the world, we have received the
> Spirit that comes from God, to teach us to understand the gifts
> that he has given us. (1 Corinthians 2:12)

If only we could come to understand life as a gift, it would be
conversion enough. And how that understanding would transform our teaching and learning. But as it is, we regard the
world and the objects of our knowledge as things to be seized,
possessed, and owned.

We speak about "pursuing truth" as if it were a quarry to
be hunted down, and that usage is not accidental: we seek
to know things so we can master them, own them, change
them, control them. And with our knowledge, we often proceed to brutalize the world—witness our relationship to nature
and the ecological catastrophe we have triggered. When we
treat the world not as a gift but as plunder, we destroy the gift
we have been given—a gift that would sustain us if we would
only receive it in gratitude and humility.

When we fail to receive truth as gift but pursue it and
wrestle it down, surely the quality of our knowledge suffers.
For if truth is personal, then truth, like a person, will not
reveal itself as fully to one who tries to pry it open as to one
who waits and listens with attention and respect. The kind of
truth that matters does not make itself known to those who
shout for it to come out and then try to batter down the door.

The truth that matters must trust us before we can have a relationship with it.

Perhaps our problem in receiving truth as a gift is that every gift makes us dependent on the giver, especially the gift of life. When we accept such a large gift, we feel a debt and an obligation, which goes against the grain of our desire for independence and autonomy. Indeed, the very reason we wish to learn, the basis on which we sell education in our society, is that knowledge increases our ability to go it alone, lessening the likelihood that we will be dependent on anyone. Modern education is training for autonomy, and in that context, it is almost impossible to admit that knowledge itself is a gift!

But the fact is that we are dependent, whether we know it or not or like it or not, and authentic knowledge both requires and generates the humility and gratitude that our dependence implies. Far from the false pride and arrogance of power that a "higher education" sometimes instills, authentic education helps us understand that everything we have is sheer gift— and that a gift is to be enjoyed and shared, not used to seek dominion.

IX

Therefore we teach, not in the way in which philosophy is taught, but in the way the Spirit teaches us: we teach spiritual things spiritually. (1 Corinthians 2:13)

Paul suggests that the relation of teacher to learner should be like the Spirit's relation to us. If we want to teach that way, we must understand the Spirit's own ways of teaching.

One way is the way of freedom: the word of truth is spoken, and we are free to choose whether to hear it or not. If we hear it, we are free to choose whether to follow it or not. The response is ours, but no matter what our response may be, the word is continually spoken, a word of freedom spoken in freedom.

The Spirit does not coerce us into listening or following, and good teachers will not coerce their students. This is a fundamental challenge in a mandatory system of schooling, amplified by the pressure of grading. But where there is no freedom, no real learning can occur. Whether we know it or not, acknowledge it or not, like it or not, students will always choose whether or not to learn. Authentic education raises that fact to consciousness and blesses it instead of ignoring or resisting the inevitable.

Second, the Spirit teaches us in love. The freedom that God gives us is not a sign of indifference; we are not ignored or abandoned in our freedom. The Spirit yearns for us to use our freedom to follow in truth's way, a way that leads to the greatest freedom of all, freedom from death-in-life. But if we reject that way and enslave ourselves to a living death, the Spirit remains with us: God's love persists, beckoning us out of dark places into the light. So it must be with teacher and learner. Despite the rejections and rebuffs that teachers experience from students, the true teacher is one who persists in evoking the "better angels" of each student's nature, doing so in the spirit of love.

Third, the Spirit teaches us in truth. God is the great unmasker of illusions, the great destroyer of icons and idols. God's love for us is so great that God does not want us to harbor false images, no matter how much false comfort they bring us. God strips falsehood from us no matter how naked it may leave us, because it is better to live naked in truth than clothed in fantasy. So it is with the true teacher who loves his or her students too much to permit untruth to go unchallenged. Dostoevsky said it succinctly and well: "Love in action is a harsh and dreadful thing compared with love in dreams."[3]

X

An unspiritual person is one who does not accept anything of the Spirit of God; he sees it all as nonsense; it is beyond his understanding because it can only be understood by means of the Spirit. A spiritual man, on the other hand, is able to judge the value of everything, and his own value is not to be judged by other men. (1 Corinthians 2:14–15)

Here Paul focuses on the student and on his or her readiness to understand truth. Teaching, Paul reminds us, is not a one-way street, and the spirit of true teaching must be matched by a spirit of receptiveness inside the learner. The same Spirit that is at work in the teacher must be at work in the student, or no conversation can occur.

So as learners, we must pray for openness to that Spirit, for a receptiveness to truth that may not come naturally to even the most brilliant mind. And as teachers, we must not only make room for the Spirit to move within us but also cultivate learning situations that will help students open up to that movement. We must trust that every student has the capacity to receive the Spirit, that there is, as the Quakers say, "that of God" in every person. Then we must create classroom environments that bring out that often hidden potential.

Such an environment will be cooperative, not competitive; it will help us seek each other's strengths and build on them rather than ferret out weaknesses to exploit. Such an environment will reward those who acknowledge ignorance as well as those who give correct answers, for only as we reveal our not-knowing can we discover what we need to know. Such an environment will honor the whole person, not just the disembodied mind, for the Spirit speaks to our hearts as well as to our intellects.

When we achieve receptiveness to the Spirit, we are, as Paul says, "able to judge the value of everything." What an extraordinary definition of authentic education! What the educated person needs to know is not the appearance of a thing, which is readily available to our eyes and ears, but the value of a thing and its meaning in our lives, that which no eye has seen and no ear has heard.

The man or woman who knows the value of things is one whose own value "is not to be judged" by other persons. Of course not! Such a person has no need to ask his or her worth in the eyes of others; such a person will know that he or she has ultimate worth simply by virtue of being human. The God who comes into our lives as a plumb line, showing us the value of all things, is a God who says to each of us, no matter what our condition, "You are loved." To be educated truly and well is, above all else, to know this.

XI

As scripture says: "Who can know the mind of the Lord, so who can teach him?" But we are those who have the mind of Christ. (1 Corinthians 2:16)

"We are those who have the mind of Christ." How arrogant the claim sounds! Yet it is not a claim made in human pride. It is made, instead, on the basis of God's incarnation in Jesus, made on the basis of God's word become flesh. If the incarnation—the mystery of a being both human and divine—means anything, it means that "the mind of Christ" is a mind that mortals can take on. The scandal of the Christian profession is that God took on mortality in order that mortals could take on God's life.

For Christian teachers and learners, Paul has been spelling out the meaning of the mind of Christ throughout the second chapter of his first letter to the church at Corinth. In teaching and learning, as in every aspect of our lives, we are invited to have the mind of Christ. In the generosity and grace of that mind, education is converted from training us in technique to deepening us in wisdom, renewing in turn our knowledge, our persons, our relationships, our world.

NOTES

Introduction to the 2008 Edition

1. Richard Hughes, *How Christian Faith Can Sustain the Life of the Mind* (Grand Rapids, Mich.: Eerdmans, 2001), p. 142.

2. For information on Pendle Hill, go to www.pendlehill.org.

3. Henri J. M. Nouwen, *Reaching Out: The Three Movements of the Spiritual Life* (New York: Doubleday, 1975).

4. I have edited the new edition of this book for style, but I have tried to leave my 1980 ideas intact. Having spent the past thirty years trying to learn how to write, an ongoing task, I am incapable of publishing a line when I can see a way to make it a bit clearer and more graceful, even when what it says makes me squirm.

5. Anne Lamott, "Breaking the Surface," www.salon.com/columnists/lamott.html.

6. These words are attributed to Bohr in many secondary sources, though I have been unable to find them in his published works.

But their authenticity is largely confirmed by a remark made by his son, Hans Bohr, in an essay called "My Father": "One of the favorite maxims of my father was the distinction between the two sorts of truths, profound truths recognized by the fact that the opposite is also a profound truth, in contrast to trivialities where opposites are obviously absurd." S. Rozental, ed., *Niels Bohr: His Life and Work as Seen by His Friends and Colleagues* (New York: Wiley, 1967), p. 328.

7. William James, *The Varieties of Religious Experience* (New York: Longman, 1902), p. 49.

Chapter I: In the Belly of a Paradox

1. Thomas Merton, *The Sign of Jonas* (New York: Harcourt, 1953), p. 11.

2. Thomas Merton, *A Thomas Merton Reader*, ed. Thomas P. McDonnell (Garden City, N.Y.: Image Books, 1974), p. 16.

3. Thomas Merton, *Zen and the Birds of Appetite* (New York: New Directions, 1968), p. 140.

4. "Magic Penny" (also known as "Love Is Something"), words and music by Malvina Reynolds, copyright © 1955 and 1986 Northern Music Corporation, renewed in 1986.

5. Thomas Merton, *Conjectures of a Guilty Bystander* (New York: Doubleday, 1966), pp. 12–13.

6. Thomas Merton, "Conscience of a Christian Monk," audiotape (Chappaqua, N.Y.: Electronic Paperbacks, 1972).

7. Ibid.

8. Thomas Merton, *The Asian Journal* (New York: New Directions, 1973), pp. 335–336.

9. Thomas Merton, *The Way of Chuang Tzu* (New York: New Directions, 1969), p. 65.

10. Merton, *Conjectures of a Guilty Bystander*, p. 73.

11. Thomas Merton, "Contemplation in a World of Action" (New York: Doubleday, 1971), p. 164.

12. Merton, *The Way of Chuang Tzu*, p. 107.

13. Merton, *Zen and the Birds of Appetite*, pp. 103–104.

14. Quoted in Elizabeth Watson, *This I Know Experimentally* (Philadelphia: Friends General Conference, 1977), p. 16.

15. Merton, *The Way of Chuang Tzu*, pp. 110–111.

16. Ibid., p. 31.

17. Ibid.

18. Ibid., p. 114.

19. Merton, "Conscience of a Christian Monk."

20. Ibid.

21. Ibid.

Chapter II: The Stations of the Cross

1. Loren Eiseley, *The Star Thrower* (New York: Harvest Books, 1978).

2. Rainer Maria Rilke, *Letters to a Young Poet*, trans. M. D. Herter Norton (New York: Norton, 1993), p. 35.

3. Elisabeth Kübler-Ross, *On Death and Dying* (New York: Simon & Schuster, 1969), p. 7.

4. Thomas Merton, "To Each His Darkness," in *Raids on the Unspeakable* (New York: New Directions, 1966), pp. 11–12.

5. Erich Fromm, *Escape from Freedom* (New York: Holt, Rinehart & Winston, 1941).

Chapter III: Paradoxes of Community

1. For information on Koinonia Partners, go to www.koinoniapartners .org. On the roots of Habitat for Humanity, see www.habitat.org/ how/historytext.aspx.

2. For information on the Bruderhof Communities, now known as Church Communities International, go to http://www.church communities.org.

3. The Lindisfarne Community evolved into the Lindsfarne Association; for information, go to www.williamirwinthompson.org/ lindisfarne.html. The Pendle Hill Web site is at www.pendlehill.org.

4. "To love the little platoon we belong to in society is the first principle (the germ as it were) of public affections." Edmund Burke, *Reflections on the Revolution in France* (New York: Penguin Classics, 1982), p. 135. Originally published 1790.

5. William Johnston, *Christian Zen* (New York: HarperCollins, 1971), p. 63.

Chapter IV: A Place Called Community

1. Philip Rieff, *The Triumph of the Therapeutic* (New York: HarperCollins, 1966).

2. C. Wright Mills, *The Causes of World War Three* (New York: Simon & Schuster, 1958).

3. Dietrich Bonhoeffer, *Life Together* (New York: HarperCollins, 1978), pp. 26–27.

4. Richard Sennett, *The Uses of Disorder* (New York: Norton, 1992), ch. 2.

5. Martin Buber, *Between Man and Men* (London: Routledge, 2002), p. 9.

6. See Parker J. Palmer, *The Company of Strangers* (New York: Crossroad, 1983).

7. A good example is "Lost on the Moon," a simulation game described by Jay Hall in "Decisions," *Psychology Today*, Nov. 1971, pp. 51 ff. See also CSAP Institute for Partnership Development, "Involvement Activity A.3: The Moon Walk," preventiontraining.samhsa.gov/cti02/17h-Cda3.htm.

8. Mildred Binns Young, *What Doth the Lord Require of Thee?* Pamphlet no. 145 (Wallingford, Pa.: Pendle Hill, 1966).

9. Ibid.

Chapter V: A World of Scarcity, a Gospel of Abundance

1. During the academic year 1994–95, I served as the Eli Lilly Visiting Professor at Berea College in Berea, Kentucky. Founded in 1855 to provide a higher education for the young people of Appalachia, Berea charges no tuition but involves students in various forms of work to enhance their education and help keep the institution afloat. Fifteen years after writing these words, it was good to see with my own eyes that some of what I had written about could be found outside the pages of a book!

Chapter VI: The Conversion of Knowledge

1. Alfred North Whitehead, *The Aims of Education* (New York: Free Press, 1967), p. 14.

2. See Acts 9:1–20.

3. Fyodor Dostoevsky, *The Brothers Karamazov* (New York: Signet Classics, 1999), p. 66. Originally published 1879.

THE AUTHOR

PARKER J. PALMER is a highly respected writer, speaker, workshop leader, and activist who focuses on issues in education, community, leadership, spirituality, and social change. His work speaks deeply to people in many walks of life, including public schools, college and universities, religious institutions, corporations, foundations, and grassroots community groups.

Palmer served for fifteen years as senior associate of the American Association of Higher Education. He now serves as senior adviser to the Fetzer Institute. He founded the Center for Courage & Renewal, which oversees the "Courage to Teach" program for K–12 educators across the country and parallel programs for people in other professions, including medicine, law, ministry, and philanthropy (see www.CourageRenewal.org).

He has published a dozen poems, more than one hundred essays, and seven books, including several best-selling and award-winning titles: *A Hidden Wholeness, Let Your Life Speak, The Courage to Teach, The Active Life, To Know as We Are Known, The Company of Strangers,* and *The Promise of Paradox.*

Palmer's work has been recognized with ten honorary doctorates, two Distinguished Achievement Awards from the National Educational Press Association, an Award of Excellence from the Associated Church Press, and major grants from the Danforth Foundation, the Lilly Endowment, and the Fetzer Institute.

In 1993, Palmer won the national award of the Council of Independent Colleges for Outstanding Contributions to Higher Education. In 1998, the Leadership Project, a national survey of ten thousand administrators and faculty, named Parker Palmer one of the thirty "most influential senior leaders" in higher education and one of the ten key "agenda setters" of the decade, stating, "He has inspired a generation of teachers and reformers with evocative visions of community, knowing, and spiritual wholeness."

In 2001, Carleton College gave Palmer the Distinguished Alumni Achievement Award. In 2002, the Accreditation Council for Graduate Medical Education created the Parker J. Palmer Courage to Teach Award, given annually to the directors of ten medical residency programs that exemplify patient-centered professionalism in medical education.

In 2003, the American College Personnel Association named Palmer a Diamond Honoree for outstanding contributions to the field of student affairs. In 2005, Jossey-Bass published *Living the Questions: Essays Inspired by the Work and Life of Parker J. Palmer,* written by notable practitioners in a variety of fields, including medicine, law, philanthropy, politics, economic development, and K–12 and higher education.

Palmer received a Ph.D. in sociology from the University of California at Berkeley. A member of the Religious Society of Friends (Quaker), he lives with his wife, Sharon Palmer, in Madison, Wisconsin.

Also by Parker Palmer

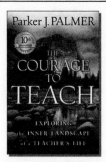

The Courage to Teach
*Exploring the Inner Landscape of a
Teacher's Life, 10th Anniversary Edition*

Parker J. Palmer

Hardcover/CD
ISBN: 978-0-7879-9686-4

*"This book is for teachers who have good days and bad—and whose bad
days bring the suffering that comes only from something one loves. It is for
teachers who refuse to harden their hearts, because they love learners,
learning, and the teaching life."*
— Parker J. Palmer [from the Introduction]

In the tenth anniversary edition of his classic *The Courage to Teach*, Parker
J. Palmer offers hope, encouragement, and guidance to teachers—and other
professionals—who want to recover the heart of their vocation and calling.
His new Foreword reflects on ten years of "courage work," which has spread
beyond education to help teachers and other professionals recover meaning
and depth in their work lives. And a new concluding chapter takes a fresh
look at a new kind of professional and what it means to "take heart" in one's
work.

BONUS: Includes an audio CD featuring a 45-minute conversation between
Parker Palmer and his colleagues Marcy Jackson and Estrus Tucker from the
Center for Courage & Renewal (www.CourageRenewal.org). They reflect on
what they have learned from working with thousands of teachers in their
"Courage to Teach" program and with others who yearn for greater integrity
in their professional lives.

The Courage to Teach Guide for Reflection and Renewal, 10th Anniversary Edition

Parker J. Palmer and Megan Scribner

Paper/DVD
ISBN: 978-0-7879-9687-1

An important text and audio-visual resource from the best-selling author of *The Courage to Teach* for readers who want to "explore the inner landscape of a teacher's life" in ways that will make a difference for them, their students, their colleagues, and their institutions.

This extensively updated and expanded Guide will help readers, individually and in groups, reflect on their teaching and renew their sense of vocation. The Guide proposes practical ways to create "safe space" for honest reflection and conversation, and offers chapter-by-chapter questions and exercises to explore the many insights in *The Courage to Teach*.

BONUS DVD: Brings *The Courage to Teach* alive through a 70-minute interview with Parker J. Palmer, originally recorded as a resource for the Center for Courage & Renewal (www.CourageRenewal.org). Here he reflects on a wide range of subjects—including the heart of the teacher, the crisis in education, diverse ways of knowing, relationships in teaching and learning, spirituality in education, approaches to institutional transformation, and teachers as culture heroes. Discussion questions related to the topics explored on the DVD have been integrated into the Guide, giving individuals and study groups a chance to have "a conversation with the author" as well as an engagement with the text.

Also by Parker Palmer

Let Your Life Speak:
Listening for the Voice of Vocation

Parker J. Palmer

Hardcover
ISBN: 978-0-7879-4735-4

A Compassionate and Compelling Meditation on Discovering Your Path in Life

With wisdom, compassion, and gentle humor, Parker J. Palmer invites us to listen to the inner teacher and follow its leadings toward a sense of meaning and purpose. Telling stories from his own life and the lives of others who have made a difference, he shares insights gained from darkness and depression as well as fulfillment and joy, illuminating a pathway toward vocation for all who seek the true calling of their lives.

"Parker Palmer's writing is like a high country stream—clear, vital, honest. If your life seems to be passing you by, or you cannot see the way ahead, immerse yourself in the wisdom of these pages and allow it to carry you toward a more attentive relationship with your deeper, truer self." **—John S. Mogabgab, editor, *Weavings Journal***

"An exuberant and passionate book. I was deeply moved and I cannot, nor do I want to, shake off the haunting questions that it raises for me. This book penetrates the soul, and it will definitely stir you to explore more of your own inner territory. What an extraordinary achievement." **—Jim Kouzes, coauthor, *The Leadership Challenge* and *Encouraging the Heart*; chairman, Tom Peters Group/Learning Systems**

A Hidden Wholeness:
The Journey Toward an Undivided Life

Parker J. Palmer

Hardcover
ISBN: 978-0-7879-7100-7

A BookSense Pick, September 2004

"This book is a treasure—an inspiring, useful blueprint for building safe places where people can commit to 'act in every situation in ways that honor the soul.' " —*Publishers Weekly*

"The soul is generous: it takes in the needs of the world. The soul is wise: it suffers without shutting down. The soul is hopeful: it engages the world in ways that keep opening our hearts. The soul is creative: it finds its way between realities that might defeat us and fantasies that are mere escapes. All we need to do is to bring down the wall that separates us from our own souls and deprives the world of the soul's regenerative powers." —**From** *A Hidden Wholeness*

In *A Hidden Wholeness*, Parker J. Palmer reveals the same compassionate intelligence and informed heart that shaped his best-selling books, *Let Your Life Speak* and *The Courage to Teach*. Here he speaks to our yearning to live undivided lives—in a world filled with the forces of fragmentation. *A Hidden Wholeness* weaves together four themes: the shape of an integral life, the meaning of community, teaching and learning for transformation, and nonviolent social change.

Defining a "circle of trust" as "a space between us that honors the soul," Palmer shows how people in settings ranging from friendship to organizational life can support each other on the journey toward living "divided no more." The hundreds of thousands of people who know Parker J. Palmer's books will be glad to find the journey continued here—and readers new to his work will be glad they joined that journey.